DARK SIDE

DARK SIDE

TRUE STORIES FROM A TEENAGE POT SMUGGLER

Stu Stall

© Stu Stall Stories LLC 2024
All Rights Reserved

No part of this book may be reproduced or transmitted in any form or by any means, electronic or mechanical, including photocopy, recording, or by any information storage and retrieval system, without the author's written permission.

ISBN: 9798989129737 (Hardback)
ISBN: 9798989129744 (Paperback)
ISBN: 9798989129751 (E-book)

Library of Congress control number 2024922929

Judy Jordan: My first friend. You were a beautiful woman in more ways than one.

TABLE OF CONTENTS

About the Author (Foreword)..I

Thirty Pieces of Silver..1

Consanguineousness Island Style...9

Snitch City..12

The War on Drugs..15

Penitence..20

The Ghetto..27

Hurricane Jane..33

Panting Patty...36

Dining With the Bros...39

Stepping Into the Shade...44

Surf Ghetto..45

The Steel Curtain...48

Luki..50

Coronado Surfers Rule...52

Sister Sue..55

The White Whale...57

Hungry Surfer Boys...59

BeBop..61

Ensenada Jail..63

Paul Bro..67

No More Chowder...70

Krishna Mulvaney's	73
Going, Going, Gone	76
The Mongoose	79
The Dark Side Rises	87
Party Time	93
Garage Sailing	99
It's Getting Dark	101
You Can Bank on That	108
M	112
The Beach Cottage	115
Betsy B	117
Big Wave Surfer	119
Island Magic	131
Two Geeks	136
I Should Have Known Better	142
Set Up	145
Smuggling	150
Mike Eats It	156
Sea Rays	158
Mazatlan Revisited	162
Brake Shoes	167
Yellow River	172
Rosarito Beach Hotel or Bust	176
Flatfoots	179
Cardiff or Bust	183
Santa Cruz	185
The Split	188
Eating Spit	192

Fish Harbor	194
More Spit	201
Snakree	205
I'll Never Know for Sure	207
Five Pieces of Silver	210
Paul Acree Grows Ears and a Tail	212
Starting at the Bottom Again	217
The System	220
Finding the Bottom	226
Round Two	229
Redemption	231
Some Things Never Change	233
The Primrose Labyrinth	236
Postscript	241

ABOUT THE AUTHOR
FOREWORD

From the author of *Hell House: True Stories from the Redheaded Stepchild* comes a new riveting batch of stories about growing up in the 1970s in Coronado, California. Being just ten miles from the Mexican border, a lot of wild things happened, like smuggling marijuana, crazy parties, girls, surfing, and all the insane stuff we used to do that you can't do any more.

I wrote this book to shed a little light on what really happened during my drug smuggling days, especially how my group interacted with some of the other smugglers. This is my story. It's a voice for the voiceless, for all those people who were lost, the casualties of *The War on Drugs*. It's also my attempt to set the record straight about all the trials and tribulations of those wild times.

The War on Drugs permeated society on all levels and made everything in the drug world worse. It led young people to rebuke social norms, turn on, tune in, drop out wasn't just a saying, people actually did it. In the 1970s, they become known as lawless degenerates, but today we might

ABOUT THE AUTHOR
FOREWORD

better call them "vanguards" in the movement to legalize marijuana.

This book is the second in a series. To really understand my journey and the journey of those around me, you need to read *Hell House: True Stories from the Redheaded Stepchild*. That book covers the childhood experiences that led me to be exploited, manipulated, and coerced. Even though I was the one taken advantage of, ultimately it was I who made the decisions to become a teenage pot smuggler and live in the wild for four years.

This second book details my short-lived pot smuggling career, which ended abruptly…and not by choice. It's about all those people who were led down the primrose path and into a life they couldn't escape, how it stole their youth and left them with bad reputations and little real world skills. The inability to change, which is the root cause recidivism, was a huge factor because that's how people viewed themselves.

When your glory years are spent being a pot smuggler and you have money and drugs and lots of sex, it's hard to turn over a new leaf. Those of us who did are the survivors; those who couldn't, well, most are no longer with us.

THIRTY PIECES OF SILVER

It had been a great morning. The surf was perfect. Now, I was resting before work began. I'd been working as a waiter and *maître d'* at Chez, a French restaurant, while attending college. Just then the phone rang. It was Judy Jordan, my dearest and most treasured friend from childhood. I would do anything for Judy. She was my favorite person since I was a kid. Sure, I had buddies at school and in sports, but when I was on my block, I was usually with Judy. Not only did I love her, but my sisters loved her and my mom loved her; she was part of the family.

More than a big sister, Judy was my best friend. She taught me how to dance and so many other things about life too. Her dad dressed her in boy's clothing and called her a tomboy, but she was super pretty. I don't know if they were her brother's old clothes (Navy guys were notoriously cheap) or if he was trying to protect her from the boys. All I know is he had to know how beautiful she was.

As the years went on we became slightly estranged, but our bond remained strong. Judy had a disastrous marriage when she was younger and ended up staying with me for a couple of months when she was down and out. She just showed up one day, and there was no way I could say no to her. I wouldn't let her sleep with me, however, even though she wanted to (as I still thought of her more as a sister).

I, Stuart Stall, did not let one of the most beautiful women I ever met in my life sleep with me. I still don't know why. I guess I wanted to keep the status quo. But only a couple of years later, when I had a safe house in Cardiff, I acquiesced and had a night I will cherish for the rest of my existence.

It started with a phone call.

"Hello."

"Hi, Stuart."

"Hi Judy. Nice to hear your voice."

"Nice to hear yours too, Stuart. I just saw Eddie O and Lights up here in Santa Barbara."

"I figured that's where they were," and that was true. At the time, Eddie Otero was a fugitive, and Bob Lahodny (aka "Lights") was on probation. Neither of them was supposed to be with a fugitive.

Judy admitted, "I told them they have to give me some money."

"Not a real good idea" I responded

"They said they would."

"Really?"

"Yeah, Eddie has a house in Monterey, they're going to fly me up there on a private plane and give me some money."

"Don't get on the plane. Whatever you do, don't get on the plane. "

"Why not?"

"You might take off with them but won't land with them. Once they get out over the ocean, they're going to throw you out."

"No, they're not, Phil's coming."

Philip DeMassa was their attorney. She used to work for him and stayed at his house. I know he loved her. All those attorneys did.

"He's one of them. He's not coming to save you; he's coming to seal your fate. He's the closer."

"What should I do then?"

"Come down here; I'll take care of you for a while."

"No, then they'll come after you."

"No, they won't. I'll make you disappear, and then we can make a deal with Phil. whatever you do, don't get on that plane."

"Okay, Stu, I got to go."

"Where are you?"

"I'm at the airport."

"Please don't get on the plane, Judy."

"I got to go, Stuart."

"I love you."

"I love you too, Stuart."

I got off the phone with Judy and instantly called Phil's office. I had the number memorized. Phil wasn't at his office, but they gave me his car phone number and called it immediately. He didn't answer, so I left this message: "Don't you dare touch one hair on her head." I hung up, laid down on my couch, and cried.

I don't know if she didn't believe me or if she was trapped. She was already at the airport and Phil wasn't answering his phone. Maybe she just went for the money or believed people she knew all her life would never do this to her. I'll never know.

Her body washed up two days later in Ventura Harbor. She was 29 years old. I'd been in love with her since I was three.

Back waiting tables at the Chez, where Phil DeMassa and Jack Palladino were regular customers. About two weeks after Judy's murder, a guy comes in for dinner. He's alone, and very early. He asks, "Are you Stuart Stall?"

"Yes," I reply.

"I have a contract on you."

I knew immediately what it was for: the message I left on Phil's phone. I'd do it again in a heartbeat, I didn't leave my name, but they knew my relationship with Judy, plus I have a distinctive voice.

"Look," he said, "I'm not going to fulfill this contract because I owe your father a favor." He paused for a minute. "Now, you owe me a favor. Deal?"

"Deal," I said.

I never saw him again until the tenth annual Jimmy Reilly Memorial Surf Contest. I was the original chairman who ran the contest and carried it on my back for the first ten years. That day, he showed up with Bob Lahodny. It had been twelve years, so he reminded me of his marker. I told him: "It's all over now,"

"Well," he responded, "it's not over 'til I collect the debt."

"No, it's over. Go ask Bob." Things escalated. At that point, we were in each other's faces. I pointed at Lahodny and again said "Go ask Bob." Finally, he went over to Bob, and they chatted adamantly while looking at me, and I was staring back. It looked resolved.

I always wondered what the favor was that my dad did for him and what he thought I would do for him to even the marker. The company had a hitman for a reason.

All of these events—Judy's murder by plane, the mark on me, the bargaining for my life—all of it had to be approved by Lou Villar, head of the Coronado Company, their boss and coincidentally my tenth-grade Spanish teacher. I'd been out of the business for four years when the hitman showed up; the business was still trying to kill me, but I had an out and the deal transpired until the marker died.

Not everyone would be so lucky.

Years later, when I did the favor of a lifetime for a local contractor (reciprocity is too big a word for him), I asked him about Judy. He was tight friends with Eddie Otero and Lights, two principals in the Coronado Company pot smuggling ring, and he knew of my connection to them.

He laughed. "They opened up the door on the plane and asked Judy if she could fly. Then Frank Cooney threw her out." Then he laughed again. He was Italian and friends with all the other Italians in Coronado. So, I told him: "You know Judy was adopted, and Mike Napolitano Sr. was her real dad."

He looked at me hard: "Really?"

I said, "I thought you would know that with all your Italian connections in town."

That shut him up. It was about time. He and his buddies had been laughing about this murder for years. The killers always wanted to recapture a slice of the euphoria they felt when they first murdered Judy and apparently bragged about it when they were partying with friends. Phil, of course, got his *thirty pieces of silver.*

Those swashbuckling, swaggering pot smugglers/killers were so tough it took three of them plus their sweet-talking attorney and a pilot to kill a ninety-eight-pound woman. Plus, they still had to deceive her to get the job done. Real tough guys.

There was no reason to kill her. Sure, she made a mistake hitting them up for money, but plenty of other people knew they were there as well. There was a large conglomeration of former Coronado people living in Santa Barbara. They could have just said no, had Phil talk to her, or they could have called me. They all knew my bond with her, especially Phil. I would have done anything to save her. I would have kept her quiet, too.

An old girlfriend once asked me, "Why would she call you?" Simple: Because she knew I loved her and would virtually do anything for her.

I've thought about it since then. I think it's also because I'm the closest thing to family that Judy ever had. I was the only one she could truly trust. She knew I loved her and that my sisters loved her. Even now, although she's been dead for forty-three years, I still love her.

CONSANGUINEOUSNESS ISLAND STYLE

This is how incestuous Coronado was at the time.

Eddie O, I've known him all my life. We were in the same class and we're the same age. Judy was two classes above us, but she also knew him for a long time. Ed was the junior high bully until my future stepbrother beat him up in front of all his greaser friends. Ed would soon drop them and become a high school waterman, Water polo, swimming, life guard, but not a dedicated surfer.

Bob Lahodny, or Lights, lived in an apartment over the garage at his mom's house on Tenth and Adella. His stepdad was the city manager of Coronado. We lived half a block away on Adella when I had my paper route. Bob fancied himself a ladies' man. He was handsome with blue eyes and relatively athletic. A few times when I got up at five in the morning for my paper route, I would see a bunch of guys passed out on Bob's lawn and parkway, and a few times in the gutter. I would ride my bike quietly, balancing the basket full of papers over my handlebars, to check them out. Judy's future husband George and ugly Frank Cooney were there. I could name the others, too, but most of them are dead.

Ugly Frank Cooney, Bob's lackey, grew up in the second house from Fourth and J Avenues. Judy grew up in a house at Fourth and I (three houses between them). We lived on I Avenue, half a block away from Judy, 'til our mom got killed. Frank had a brother my age both had known Judy, and me, their entire lives. I never liked him; he was creepy. I don't know what happened to Frank. He set them up and turned state's evidence against Eddie and Lights right after they got out of prison the first time. The Feds had Frank on ice. I know someone warned Eddie that Frank disappeared with a load (me), but he didn't listen—and it cost him, and Lights, too. I later heard those passed-out guys by Bob's pad were shooting vodka; they were probably sharing needles as most of them died from hepatitis C, including Bob and Judy's ex and probably Frank too.

I kind of liked those guys too (well, except Frank). One time, when I was eighteen, I hitchhiked to Santa Cruz. I went up there to visit Buddy, one of the Bros (aka the Cats). We went to Felton with two girls. I was underage but got in any way with my fake ID. We saw Jessie Collin Young playing in this cozy little club. Lights was there, and lots of people were drinking on his tab, so we joined them. He never knew! We had a lot of fun, and I'll never forget how generous Bob was. Whenever I got a drink, I looked for Lights, held up my drink, and said, "Yeah," trying to get his acknowledgment. It was a fun trip.

Two other Coronado guys, Don and Bo, lived across the street from the surf break *Sewer Peak*. You could sit at their table, smoke weed and watch the surf 'til you were ready to go out. I brought my wet suit, but it was bitterly cold and I was freezing ass off, but the waves were good and the cold quickly faded. I had borrowed a board and had a ton of fun.

SNITCH CITY

I totally swore off doing anything in the business after I got busted. I had two felonies and with a third I would be facing thirty years to life in prison. I didn't trust anyone in the business, which was smart. We, the fraternity of Coronado pot smugglers, all had targets on our backs, double bull's-eyes if you already had a record. Many people made into big-time dealers by prosecutors after they get busted. Cali cartel lieutenants when they were small fries, street-level dealers, or sometimes nobodies just coaxed by a friend with the enticement of quick riches (The American Dream).

A couple of years after I swore off smuggling, a girlfriend I liked a lot was getting busted, and she was the one who made the call to me. I knew it right away. It was a set up. It might have worked too, had I not already decided to give up the life. The guys who put her up to it were cunning, and likely the whole thing was fictious bait, a setup simply to ensnare me. I would have gone out of my way to help her, but I knew it was a trap. In the end, she went to prison, not me. She was just a secretary. She broke the law, but she wasn't a criminal. Plus, she had an old, longtime bad news boyfriend, and I assume one of his old connections made her an offer she couldn't refuse. I don't know. Like most people, she could have used the money. I can't blame her.

I knew the cops forced her to make the call, which hurts even though they weren't successful. I liked her a lot, but I could never trust her again, even though she worded her request so I would know. She knew I had just pled guilty to my second pot smuggling felony earlier that year, and that I was out of the business. I would have gotten a stiff sentence, probably thirty years, maybe life. So, that call was it. I was done and had been for the last two years.

See, that's how you get set up: You spend so much time with these guys that you let your guard down. To get set up, the closer the person is to the mark, the higher the degree of probability of success.

This kind of "fictitious bait" is how law enforcement made criminals out of ordinary people in the seventies and eighties. Most people I know fell into this trap. I've personally risked my own freedom to save people who were getting ready to fall into the jaws of our flawed legal system. Most of these people went on to have successful careers; some even became lawyers and doctors.

That's what people don't understand about the drug game. You didn't have to be from the streets to get involved. Many local prominent families wanted in on the game too, to get that tax-free money. The enticement, even for straight people, was sometimes too strong to ignore. I can't tell you how many people have put me down for being an ex-smuggler who wanted to be an investor, but those kinds of double lives were happening all over the country. I know plenty of people who, at one time in their life, would have gone for the big money if they had the opportunity. It would have been so easy to fall into that trap.

All it takes is one person you trust plus the lure of easy money, and next thing you know, you're busted. This is how the War on Drugs wreaks havoc on America, ruining friendships, relationships, and businesses. We deserve better. People from all walks of life fell into these ambushes. It was and is a national disgrace. I'm not talking about myself here; I was a professional. But I can't say that I didn't get into bed with the wrong people from time to time. It was impossible not to.

They were everywhere.

THE WAR ON DRUGS

They say Afghanistan was America's longest war. That's bullshit. Richard Nixon announced a "War on Drugs" during his first term, and it's still being fought today. It has been, on all fronts, an abysmal failure. Drugs have not gone away; instead, just the opposite has happened. They have become more plentiful, more powerful, and more deadly. Nixon's War on Drugs green-lighted drug cartel tactics, just like the Volstead Act during Prohibition in the 1920s empowered the Mafia and other organized criminal groups to engage in theft, murder, and all kinds of other criminal activity.

The drug war manufactured criminals day and night. Some were really bad people to begin with, sure, but most of us were just normal kids caught up in a moment or captured in a trap trying to get rich quickly. It's the American dream. For some, the drug business was supposed to be temporary, a one-time foray that in the long run wasn't for them. But for others, it was a lifestyle, a world in which they finally fit. There wasn't fentanyl or hard drugs like that; those synthetics were created because they were cheaper to make and easier to transport—which likely wouldn't ever have happened without the War on Drugs.

There wouldn't be cartels without drugs being illegal because the drugs wouldn't be so profitable. So, this so-called *War on Drugs* changed the business. The good deal days were gone. It was less forgiving on all fronts, it was all business now. Like all wars, many people didn't survive, including three of my closest friends, even though they weren't actively working at the time. It still has a way of reaching out to you because the lifestyle and choices you made follow you, even after the statute of limitations is over and done with.

I laugh when I hear people talk about the border wall (it's a fence by the way; you can't see through a wall), innocently thinking it will stop smuggling. It's hard for me to believe that people are so naïve or uninformed.

This is how smuggling works: First, you survey the situation so you know exactly what you need to do to complete your task. You then observe whatever impediments are in your way then decide how and what you need to do to circumvent them. It's the same whether you are smuggling by land, sea or air.

It's really that simple even though it's not easy at all. Smuggling takes work. The smart ones do reconnaissance to be successful, which means all kinds of surveillance. That's how it's been for centuries.

Sometimes, authorities can slow smuggling down, but it's impossible to stop it because smugglers are great at making adjustments. That's why the *War on Drugs* will never be successful. It will always make things worse because it pays smugglers who get more organized and more ruthless. Those who survive experience so many sink or swim moments that over time improve their methods. When people do get busted, they are quickly replaced by others who, like them, were just waiting for an opportunity. When police brag that they "took down" street drug gangs, it's an empty boast. There is too much money to be made no matter what level you are on, from street level to cartel kingpin you're easily replaced.

People like to get drunk, stoned, high, inebriated, whatever you want to call it. Let's face it, humans like to get fucked up. The same goes for birds, deer, rats, and pretty much any land-based animals; they want to get a buzz and it's a naturally occurring event with fermenting fruit. It's been going on forever, and you're not going to stop it. It's okay if you want to use alcohol; society has said that's the drug of choice even though it may be the most dangerous. Still, it's okay because big business makes their political donations.

The Volstead Act tried to take booze away from average Americans and you ended up with cartel-like entities (Mafia) who sold booze instead and which are still with us today. The smarter choice would have been to legalize it and control it, which is what we need to do today with drugs. The solution to the war on drugs? Sell drugs so cheap that you put the cartels out of business, and people don't have to steal or sell their bodies to get high. You put recreational drugs under complete state control and offer education and rehabilitation with all the money you're going to save with no interdiction, criminalization, incarceration, court costs, and all the other really horrible things that the drug war has spawned. This approach would put an end to all the lives lost to the business, those who could never function or flourish as they should have.

Then we have incarceration and life after imprisonment (a record that follows you around and the prison PTSD that never gets treatment). All of this could be and should be avoided for the betterment of society with compassion and understanding. It's not a panacea for all that ails us, but it's a start that should have been initiated in 1968.

There will still be overdoses and deaths, but there will be a lot less and as time goes on; not to mention there would be an astonishing amount of us who would no longer be considered criminals. The court system, the prison system, and society would all function better with a bit of empathy for our fellow humans instead of hitting them over the head and dragging them off to be warehoused at the expense of hard-working people. Even in prison people find a way to become inebriated because it's so hard to stop when that's all you know.

PENITENCE

Coronado is a small town, even smaller back then. Everyone knew everyone, well, almost. I have another friend named Judy B, actually the secretary's older sister. She knows everyone well that I've written about so far. She asked if she could stay in my house's third-floor tower room one Fourth of July weekend. I said yes, and that weekend ended up being eight days.

The first night she came to town, she took me to dinner at Eddie O's. Bob Lahodny was there. It was intimate, just the four of us. As you might imagine, I hadn't seen those guys for a while, and it was ironic that I was showing up with a woman named Judy (just not the one that they murdered).

I was my usual pleasant self even though I was about to sit down to dinner with two guys who put a contract out on me and killed my childhood best friend. We all passed around and smoked a fat joint (maybe they thought it was a peace pipe). Still, Bob didn't say a word to me or even look at me the whole time and I kind of enjoyed that even though I didn't have much to say myself. But I love paradox. I sat there with my stupid pot-smoking grin, thinking about my girl and I'm sure they could feel it. They both loved the Judy I came with. I thought they loved the other Judy, too. Bob was in her wedding as the groom was one of those guys passed out on his old front lawn. But me...I loved both Judys.

About two weeks after that dinner, Eddie showed up at my house. He brought his wife, some fish, and a fat joint. I took the fish and smoked the doobie with him. It was a peace pipe moment for Ed, but not for me (I'd already made my peace with the whole thing--sort of unwillingly, but something I needed to do). For me, it was a keep your friends close and your enemy's closer moment.

Then Ed was slightly contrite with me using words I understood, but his wife would not. I didn't say anything. I didn't want it to be misconstrued as an acceptance. I can forgive, but some things you can never forget. And I'm not that forgiving when it comes to my first girl and her murder, not to mention the hitman episode.

One of my dear friends married Phil. I went to the wedding reception with my significant other, the mother of my last two boys. In introducing herself to Phil she said, "Hi, I'm Ronda."

"I know who you are."

The wordsmith made sure she wasn't comfortable (it wouldn't have bothered me at all. I'd made my peace, and I actually liked Phil), plus I'd laugh and wordsmith him back. My world and my relationships are usually complicated, but I'm living my life every day.

It was Phil's second wedding. I didn't go to the first one, but I heard there was a shitload of smugglers there. They partied for three days, including Judy B. Ironically, I was the only smuggler at the second wedding, which was populated by all the attorneys I got to meet in the 70s when I was going to court. The guest list even included famous private detective Jack Palladino.

Phil came to me during the reception and said, "I'm really glad to see you here. I mean it, I'm REALLY glad you're here."

An apology for the hitman! It's almost like he had a conscience (just kidding). If I thought I needed to say something to my friend, the bride, I would have, but I didn't. I didn't let that or anything else stop me from having a good time. I danced with my goddaughter, her mom, and my girlfriend. I had great conversations with the two attorneys I'd known for a long time. I'm sure many of those attorneys were thinking what was I doing there, and I wondered how many knew what happened to Judy.

Phil and his bride attended one of my Christmas parties at my mini-mansion in Coronado. While admiring my house and the steel drum player, Phil said,

"I wish our friend could be here too."

I made him say it twice, pretending I didn't hear it the first time. I could feel a temporary pall come over me, but I quickly recovered.

"She called me from the Santa Barbara airport. I told her exactly what was going to happen to her."

Neither one of us said a thing. I let it hang there. I'm sure he was truly sorry, but we both knew what his job entailed that fateful day. "Get some food, Phil. I made it all myself." which he later complemented me on. That was the end of our conversation. He didn't stay long.

I'm glad I never killed anyone, especially someone who I loved. Phil though, he had to live with that pain, and I was glad to see that it bothered him. It was just another example of how my life and relationships can be complicated, but they are what they are and it's hard to change things. I have to live with the fact that my lifelong friend called me for help in a last-minute act of desperation and I failed her.

Phil's wife's daughter, my pal, who I love, had a big wedding with lots of attorneys (Phil's daughter somehow drowned in her bathtub. When people don't drown in their bathtubs, you never hear of this happening). She always told me I'd be the one to walk her down the aisle when she married, but in the end it was Phil. I'm sure that if I had walked her down the aisle, it would have caused much controversy at the wedding—which I would have welcomed. Instead, I was the preacher, Reverend Stu, and I officiated.

I am a man of the cloth in the Universal Life Church, dating back to my early antiwar protesting days as a conscientious objector. I'm sure that was shocking enough for the guests who knew I was the only smuggler there and amusing for them to see me as The Reverend Stu. It was a fun party, and I danced with all my girls, including my significant other.

There were a lot of attorneys. I knew a bunch of them and had some great conversations with a few. I knew a handful of those attorneys before the "Coronado 27" (the first big pot bust for the Coronado Company). It wasn't my first bust, but I wasn't in the Coronado Company. The attorneys closest to Judy Jordan and I were also some of the ones closest to Phil. It's a small world sometimes.

I went to Phil's funeral. He had a scuba diving accident or something in Hawaii. I saw all those attorneys again, including Detective to the Stars Jack Palladino. I was wearing a nice black suit with black wingtips. The attorney that did the eulogy mentioned that all the smugglers, dope dealers, and assorted criminals came the day before at the viewing, and today was for them, the lawyers. I knew I wasn't going anywhere, and when he mentioned it again, I found it quite amusing. I'd never seen him before, so he didn't know me.

When I first showed up, a real pretty blonde approached me. I never met her before and said she friends with somebody who I didn't know either. I think she thought I was an attorney and was kind of hanging around me the whole time. Later, I found out it was the first Mrs. DeMassa. I also went to the internment; I don't think they really wanted me there.

This was a group of attorneys that I mostly didn't know, but one was a good friend of my late friend Judy Jordan. We used to play doubles tennis with him and his wife. The unknowns tried to vibe me, but like I said, I didn't know them, and they certainly didn't know me. I was there for my girls: the widow, her daughter, her granddaughter (my goddaughter), and Judy. I shed some tears, but they weren't for Phil; they were for my girls.

After they finished throwing their dirt, all three turned to me for long hugs, which surprised all those attorneys. Then I chatted up the blonde (just for show) as I knew they were all watching me now. Yup, Stuart Stall was here. Then I hopped into my nice Mercedes and drove away from all those attorneys, probably for the last time—but not my girls, we're still tight.

PENITENCE

I know this story will hurt many people, but it's the only micron of justice Judy will ever get. I've loved her since I was three years old. Our bond is still strong and I still love her. All the fun I had with her from childhood to adulthood in my life, but now when I think of her, I always cry; every once in a while, you can see it, but most times I just suck it up. Here's my story of how I got caught up in the business and the consequences. It's not about the Coronado Company, but as you can see, they're in it, even though I was never in the Coronado Company.

THE GHETTO

In 1972 I was working at the Chowder House and living in the "shack" at what now was known as the Ghetto (surfer ghetto). The Ghetto had three houses, each two-bedrooms with one-bath, and the shack, a former stable with a dirt floor. That's where I lived. There was no plumbing or electricity, so we ran an extension cord from the back house. It was all pretty rudimentary. I was still driving the dune buggy I bought from Lance Weber, the one I had to push to jump-start the engine every morning because something called the solenoid got burned out. When I bought it from Lance, he told me it came with free labor but not free parts, but I had no idea where to get parts for a '49 Ford turned dune buggy. It was a fun car, even if impractical.

Two surfers from our group, The Bro's (aka the Cats), rented one of the front houses at the Ghetto, and some guy we all thought was a narc or a cop rented the other one in the front.

It was now party central all the time at the Ghetto. We only had one rule... no rules. They even had their own team in the local softball league, the Ghetto Grinders. They had the best cheer in the league: "GA G GTO ghetto, ghetto, go, go, go." It was the only cheer. I was on a different team, the Crown City Coasters, where I was the youngest guy on that team. We had no problem beating the Ghetto Grinders, but I think they had more fun. Their pitcher was a guy named Paul Acree, one of the two founders of the Coronado Company.

I was making nine dollars a day as the cook at the Chowder House, with no taxes taken out (I wasn't an official employee) as I was paid under the table. After a couple of weeks working there, management let me come to their gambling game after work. It was blackjack. They had a decent crowd. I was up over twenty dollars at one point that night, but I left with nothing, not even the nine-dollar under-the-table pay I earned that day. I needed a new strategy, so after that night, I always left the table after my first loss whenever I got up to twenty dollars. That strategy worked well; I tripled my income.

They had a thriving mini casino for about two hours after work, but not every day, but often. That was an interesting job... I was making gourmet sandwiches,

THE GHETTO

Rubens, Kosher meats and even tongue (that was nasty). The people who liked their tongue sandwiches were regulars and I think most were related. Working with the tongue was almost enough to make me quit, and I always wanted to walk through the dining room to see who was eating tongue (yuck). On Friday night, they served fish and chips, all deep fried. A bunch of colorful Coronado guys had had the job before me, like Dave Ryan, who even invented his own sandwich... "The Ryan." Well, I wasn't looking for such illustrious fame. Anyway, he comes in one day and says to me, "You know the owner screws all her cooks."

"Dave, I thought you stopped messing with me." Dave was my neighbor and older than me (I was friends with his younger brother), so he thought he could mess with us, kind of hazing the younger guys, but with Dave it was all the time. Dave himself was handsome, but some of those cooks before me were definitely not. And I'm a guy who really likes beautiful women. Actually, all of my favorites had the Judy Jordan profile: Angelic face, slender athletic body, quick wit and an extra helping of sweetness. I liked other girls, too, but this is where I usually end up. And many of those girls were cheerleaders, even though I was never on the football team. No, for me, it was surfing.

I was, and am, an avid surfer. I am even a proud owner of a beautiful Donald Takayama Nose Rider longboard. Surfing is called the sport of kings for a reason ... there's nothing more fun in this world. Jimmy Reilly and Buddy, one of my other surfer brothers, who needed a place to stay that summer. Buddy ended up rooming with me in the shack. It was an encumbrance, but I was a good Bro. When my Coronado High School class was graduating and I was not, we were all in the dune buggy, driving by the graduation ceremony at Cutler Field, when this lady, who had just parked, pulled out in front of me. I hit her with the dune buggy. I had to do a police report, and then they sued me and took me to small claims court.

Funny thing: I had never registered my name for the car because I didn't know about that stuff and Lance didn't tell me. Lance had to go to court with me because he was still on title as the legitimate owner. I told my story, and the judge asked the car's driver to tell their side. A man stood up and said his wife couldn't be here today, even though she was driving. The judge asked why not, and he said because she was indisposed. I looked at Lance and shrugged my shoulders. I didn't know what he meant by "indisposed." Lance motioned like he was drinking something from a cup and tilting his head back.

I got it, she was drunk, and the judge saw that too. If she's "indisposed" at 10 o'clock in the morning, she must be really incapacitated by 6 o'clock in the evening. I won the case because I had the right-of-way, but it was a wakeup call; the buggy wasn't doing well, so I returned the pink slip to Lance. I shouldn't have bought the car in the first place because it really needed Lance to tinker with it daily.

About two weeks later, there was a knock at the shack door. Buddy and I had been resting after surfing all morning. I opened the door. It was Judy Jordan, my pal. She had a present for me from Lance. In this big green duffel bag (or Sea Bag) she had a bunch of marijuana, maybe a pound or two; the problem was it was really wet. I took it and asked if she wanted to come in and hang out. She looked around, smiled, and said she had stuff to do. The next morning, I tied a rope around the bag, put it in my bicycle basket, and rode up to the Laundromat. It was early, and no one was in there, so I threw the sea bag in a dryer and went off to the beach.

When I returned, everything was dry, so I put it back in my basket and rode it back to the Ghetto. We put it in a large plastic bag. It was quite a bit of weed, probably over two pounds. We made a smaller bag for smoking and left the rest in the entry room, kind of stashed away. A couple nights later, in the middle of the night, a cop broke into the shack and rousted us. He found the little bag of marijuana, handcuffed us and put us in the backseat of his radio car.

I yelled and screamed about my fourth Amendment rights. There was no search warrant, there was no probable cause. He just busted in. He was the new punk cop, Officer Dimwit. There has always been a cop in Coronado who harassed teenagers, and it was usually the new cop who took it upon himself to be that punk. I bitched so much that he called his supervisor Lieutenant Black who assessed the situation and told Dimwit to let us go. We were uncuffed and let back into the shack. They took our weed, but just the little bag. The big bag was still ours.

HURRICANE JANE

The McCloud party... It was the classic Coronado party. Mrs. McCloud (aka Hurricane Jane) had left town to visit relatives, and once that became public knowledge, it was time to party on the Rock. She was a widow; her husband was a Navy test pilot killed on duty, leaving her to raise eight children by herself. It was her children who nicknamed her Hurricane Jane. I was over at the McCloud house once with her oldest son and my buddy Eddie G. We went there to smoke a joint on the third floor with John Bomb, the oldest.

The mom returned while we were smoking. Eddie G and I had to crawl out a window and sit on the third-floor roof to hide. That third-floor roof had a 30° angle, and I wasn't feeling too comfortable out there. Inside there was a category five hurricane blowing, so we had no choice. Apparently, she knew what marijuana smelled like. Later (after we crawled back in), her son told us it was just a tropical storm. Lucky us.

I decided after that I'd never go over to that house again, but not longer after, there I was and the party just getting starting. There were five kegs (which I bought) and a pool, so it didn't take long before lots of people were intoxicated and naked. I was having a fantastic time until the police showed up. I was the first to get arrested, my old friend Nancy was second.

They were escorting us out of the party via the driveway. I had one cop who had a hold of my left shoulder while naked Nancy had two cops escorting her out, she needed two cops because her tits were so big. The cop escorting me out held me very loosely by the left shoulder (I don't think he really wanted to touch me), and as soon as we got past the house, I shrugged him off my shoulder and jumped over this little wall that was maybe a foot or a foot and half high and ran.

The copper went right after me, and I could hear his shin-shattering cry as he evidently didn't notice the little wall. The two cops shepherding Nancy dropped her and took off after me, but I'm a superfast runner and unlike the cops was utterly unadorned. It must have been an unbelievable scene. I was totally naked and barefoot. I could hear the cops right behind me when I ran across a wet lawn on the corner of Eighth and 'A' Avenue. Then I ran out into the street where the cop's wet shoes didn't work so well, and I could hear them "Bam, Bam" and their equipment hitting the road. I was now laughing and still running buck naked, but I'm sure if someone was watching, they saw lots of sparks flying and were probably laughing their ass off.

It turns out the Coronado police arrested over a hundred and twenty people at that party. Still, they only got eleven of them down to the police station. Every time they arrested someone, put them in the radio car and went back to the party to get more people, someone else would come up and let them out of the cop car.

This happened over and over again, and I heard people were getting their handcuffs cut off in the middle of the night with hacksaws all over town. Not me; I ran to my friend's house and borrowed some swim trunks from his girlfriend.

I had to knock on the door in the buff. She didn't seem to mind.

I went back and stood about half a block away and watched all the mayhem, and then later, I went back and got my clothes. I don't know if Hurricane Jane ever found out about that party, but I wouldn't want to be around if she did. It would have been the first category six on record, but probably not the last with climate change upon us.

PANTING PATTY

One night my best friend Jimmy Riley and I were cruising around and ran into two girls maybe a year or two younger than us. We asked if they wanted to have some fun. They said they were up for it, and I could tell they were excited to be hanging out with a couple of good-looking, slightly older surfer boys. Expectations were high. Jimmy didn't want to take them to the ghetto (these girls were too classy) but said his dad was out of town and his mom wouldn't be home till late. So, we went over to the Riley house. Jimmy's parents had a really nice house, an Irving Gill home. He was a famous architect who built some beautiful, gorgeous Spanish homes. Jimmy took his blonde immediately upstairs, and said the brunette and I could have the dining room.

These girls were ready to go. I took the brunette into the dining room, and it wasn't long before we were naked. I found out later she was known as "Panting Patty," but I would have figured that out by myself, as I had her panting right away. We had been going at it for about half an hour when the door opened. It was Helen, Jimmy's mom. She just looked at me, and I'm sure I instantly turned red with embarrassment.

She asked, "Where's Jimmy? "

"He's upstairs," I answered, naked, red, now embarrassed as well, and she closed the door.

I was ready to get Patty panting again, but she was already dressing and through panting for the evening. It was probably all that noise that got us busted by Helen in the first place. Then Jimmy came downstairs and said, "I got my mom locked in her room."

I turned to Patty, with a big grin on my face, but she just shook her head. I laughed. I knew she was done.

In the months that followed, I would see Helen all the time, but she never said a word to me about it. She was a really good mom. I hated getting busted by Helen because she always treated me right. It was mortifying, but Helen understood. She had four older children, and three were beauty queens. I'm sure she had kept quiet many times before, and I'm pretty sure she's seen it all.

Jimmy and I found plenty of girls, but these girls get a story because it's a story. I love Helen, she was always good to me. She knew I loved her son. We were best friends since junior high. She knew I tried to keep Jimmy out of trouble, even if we both got into all kinds of trouble; she had to know I really was trying to look out for Jimmy.

DINING WITH THE BROS

Even though we weren't rich, the Bros still liked to go out and eat, probably because none of us knew how to cook much and we were really a ton of fun when we got together. One of the places we liked to go was Jalisco Café in Palm City. The palms were long gone by the time we got there, all replaced by trailer parks. They had really good Mexican food and portions large enough for these extra-hungry young Adonis-bodied surfer boys.

After a few chow down sessions, one of the Bros, Timmy Hacker, started eating a lot of cayenne pepper. (It was the 1970s; he was going metaphysical or something). Then, he started drinking salsa. So when we came in and sat down, Timmy would pick up the communal bowl of salsa that they used to leave on the table for everyone to use all day and drank the whole thing. Who knows who was eating there before or what their level of hygiene was? Anyone could have dipped anything into it.

Still, Timmy downs the salsa. When the waitress comes up to the table, Timmy cuts off her introduction and says, "Hey, we're out of salsa."

She looks at him with a look of disgust. "Oh, it's you again." The rest of us are trying not to snicker or just burst out laughing, and it's hard not to… And she knows…she's shaking her head.

Now Timmy is sweating profusely, I think because the hot peppers kicked in. He's using up all the napkins, and we have to ask for more. Again we get the look, but the food is great and we keep coming back.

We also loved going to Chu Dynasty in Coronado because they would serve us booze when we were still teenagers. We always ordered the Ruddy Rarry to drink, which was their version of a Bloody Mary. It would produce laughs and snickering when they would repeat our order.

One time, when we were eating there, one of the Bros found a moth in his chicken cashew. The waiter says, "It no cook in there; it fly in there." After we stopped laughing, Woody, the Bro with the moth, said, "It fly in there?" The waiter replied, "Yeah, it fly in there." He got a new batch, and we still went back all the time because it was good food with lots of protein and in our price range. Oh, and it was the only place we could all go out and drink, not counting Mexico.

There was also The 24-Hour Café, which became our breakfast place. Three eggs special with lots of hash browns was our go-to after early morning surf sessions. Those girls who worked there knew we were local sufers and that we were hungry, so they took care of us. The owner, Clayton Rice, was on my old paper route. His daughters were the waitresses, and he was the cook. The entire surfer boy community knew the daughters had great asses, and they had to know it too with how loud we were. They tended to bend over for us to get plates and stuff (we knew were to sit). We used to argue who they were bending over for. I must admit, I always thought it was me.

Scoob, named after his famous Navy Seal Team/UDT father and his brother, Baby Huey, started hanging out with us because we were so much fun. We were all water guys and liked to eat a lot. Their mom oversaw security on the Naval Amphibious Base in Coronado so these guys had the run of the place. Next thing you know, we're in the chow line for free on lobster night! We surfers ate a lot on that base and nobody messed with us because nobody wanted to mess with Mama Scoob. The surfers knew to stay out of her way, too. I think they were the only family to ever live on the Amphibious Base that wasn't in the Navy. Nobody in the Navy had the balls to tell Mama Scoob she had to move after her divorce.

Three times, all the surfers loaded up in three cars with lots of joints, which we'd burn on our way to the Hare Krishna Temple in Pacific Beach. We were all really loaded when we got there, and the one liners were flying as it was easy to make jokes when you have plenty of fodder. The Bros were there for free food, our unbelievable camaraderie and a good time as usual. There were fifteen of us mixing in with a dozen saffron-robed, shaved heads with little ponytail guys with bells or symbols on their fingers.

The Bros had a good time everywhere they went and this was no exception. I don't remember what we ate or if it had a name, but it was green and vegetarian, and nobody died or got sick. I think our quasi-leader at the time, Timmy Hacker, was susceptible to the cult craze going around in the 1970s. He ended up doing time in the Air Force and took us on this odyssey, I believe.

Ironically, the Hare Krishna Temple is where the drug lawyers sent their clients after they said, "If I pay your fee, my family and I are going to starve," to which the lawyers replied, "No, there's free food every evening at the Hare Krishna Temple on Grand in Pacific Beach right before you get to Cass Street."

STEPPING INTO THE SHADE

Back at the Chowder House, the owner Jane asked me if I would go with her to Tijuana in the morning before work. I agreed, and she told me she was picking up Laetrile for her husband's mother, who was dying of throat cancer. We went down to TJ and got the drugs at a regular drugstore. Then she took me to Corona Bowl and both had burritos. There, she bought me a Bohemia beer while she had a screwdriver. She said they make the best screwdrivers because they squeeze the oranges right in front of you, but the burritos were pretty good too.

I had been to Tijuana plenty of times, drinking and getting wild with the surf gang and Coronado girls as a teenager or getting crappy haircuts with my cheap ass dad when I was a kid. Now, I was smuggling cancer drugs at the request of and with my employer all for nine bucks a day. I ended up going back every other week.

SURF GHETTO

It was 1972, and all the surfers in our group were George McGovern supporters; if any of them weren't, they didn't let it be known. I even had my picture taken with McGovern at San Diego's Lindbergh Field because I was a big follower and anti-war supporter, and none of us were in favor of the Vietnam War. We had parties at the ghetto almost every weekend, and most were pretty wild. Just the other day a Coronado woman almost my age told me that she loved going over there to see all those Adonis-bodied surfer boys. We were still doing surf trips up and down the coast and almost all of us were really good surfers.

One late morning after surfing, Jimmy Reilly showed up at the ghetto with two young girls. I got the brunette, and Jimmy, as always, took the blonde. My brunette was ten times prettier than Jimmy's blonde; in fact, I thought she was absolutely gorgeous. I guess I don't know what he was thinking... blinded by the blonde, maybe? Either way, Deborah, that brunette, she eventually became my girlfriend fifteen years later. Sometimes, it's a small world.

That morning, everyone was in the shack having fun when Lance Webber appeared and commented on how young they were. (I think he was just jealous). He wanted his sea bag, which Judy had dropped off a week ago. The police Chief's daughter tried to get it from me the night before, but I didn't know she was smuggling with Lance, so I refused. Now, I understood. I got it for him, and then he asked me if I wanted to make extra money.

"Doing what?"

"Beach crew." After I declined, he asked me point blank, "How did you dry the weed?"

"In the dryer at the Laundromat."

Lance laughed. "Really? Did it smell?"

"Not really, only a little when I opened the dryer, but I closed it right away."

It wasn't the first time I'd been asked to smuggle weed. That was when I was fifteen doing my paper route. There was this older guy who also had a paper route, Mike R, and he knew I could run. He asked me if I wanted to run through Smuggler's Gulch with a backpack full of kilos. It was simple, he said, "Just follow the guy in front of you, then jump into a van, and you get one of the kilos."

The group mainly consisted of guys from the Coronado High School cross-country team, of which he was a member. He told me a few names to try and entice me into running, and I declined his offer more than once. I'd hung out at Mama Long's house sometimes, where many older Coronado smugglers lived and partied. There were and have been people in Coronado smuggling from Mexico for decades, even before I was born.

Our proximity to Mexico hasn't changed, and the opportunity can be seen just standing on the beach in Coronado. From the sand, you can see Mexico. I'd also been to Chad's Open House in Rosarito, Baja, CA. That's where Eddie Otero and Paul Acree had a house. They hired Lance to work for them after he exited prison in 1972. He brought something they didn't have: expertise. Lance was the original pied piper of smuggling in Coronado and the one who made that generation into professional smugglers. The other big recruiter for smugglers in Coronado was Lou Villar, my tenth-grade Spanish teacher and he was recruited by Lance. He started working as an employee, and Chad (the landlord) was a coyote who smuggled pollos (a human migrant smuggler).

THE STEEL CURTAIN

Late one night, after some commotion in the alley, there was a knock on the shack's door. I saw two cars in the alley, motors still running. At the door was my friend Germ; Lou Villar was in one car, and the other car was full of Pittsburgh Steelers that they'd met in Tijuana. It was the famous defensive line, The Steel Curtain, and it was all of them. Germ knew I had a massive piece of hash, and the Steelers were looking to score weed, but they couldn't find any. I had traded half the formally wet kilo for the hash, and I was a good Bro, so I gave them the hash; I knew it meant a lot to them (both parties).

A few months later, just before Christmas, Lou showed up at the shack with a check for my labor. I had scraped a house he was painting on Ocean Blvd, the one where Lance conscripted him. He then handed me a maroon sweatshirt and, I don't know why, but he made me feel creepy and uneasy, just like the time when he told me I could get a C if I didn't return to his Spanish class. I don't know what it was, but my normal defenses kicked in. Lou sure liked to hang out with the guys, and he had several groups of them, which he wanted to keep separate from each other. A few years later, when I was buying some kilos in Tijuana, the Mexican dealer called Lou a *Joto*, a Mexican Spanish slang word for a homosexual.

LUKI

Luki Pooler was the owner and landlord of the Ghetto, which she called her honeymoon cottages. From a block away, you could tell she was different, a character and a half, or maybe just crazy. She was one of a kind, almost like she was from another planet. The minute she saw Buddy's dog Rhoda (a female dog), she said, "Slut dog, she's a slut dog," and then she saw Desperate Dan and called him a Jew. Every time after that, she would see him and snarl something. You'd like to say she came from another decade or century, but she was really from another universe.

Desperate had a big nose and a darker complexion, but none of us were very religious, and we didn't care or worry about anyone's heritage or religion because the only thing we worshiped was the surf. Luki had another group of homes in San Ysidro where she lived. They were all painted the same army surplus green color that she must have gotten for free somewhere. Every time she showed up, it was a scene. We had a lot of fun making fun of Luki. We would have given her a good nickname, but her real name was already perfect.

CORONADO SURFERS RULE

The surf ghetto was a fun place to live. There is always something going on; we partied every weekend and attracted many girls. All those four and five-hour surf sessions had made all the surfers studley, plus we were a fun group with tons of great camaraderie.

Half of the surfer boys had dads I never met, but I was the one oddball missing a mom. We had a few Mamas' boys, a spoiled brat, and an admiral's son in our crew. The admiral's son had an admiral's sticker on his car, so we could cruise right on the Navy base whenever we wanted, and when they saw the stars, the Marines at the gate snapped to. That sticker allowed us to surf on the base at Erdman Beach when the South swells came in the summer. Then he welded the top of a surf trophy as a hood ornament, making it the ultimate surfer car.

Those waves were nearly perfect and almost too fast. There was no way you could drop in and take a bottom turn; you had to angle off and go, and I mean go fast, or you get eaten alive. When they had the world surfing championships in Ocean Beach in 1972, there was no surf in Ocean Beach. It was less than a foot. Coronado surfers at the same time were eating up the South swell. It was big and powerful at Erdman's, which was pumping eight to ten-foot freight trains (waves).

The local surfers knew these waves and loved them as they were the talk of legendary surf sessions. We actually waited for them every year and ripped them to shreds with our angle off-and-go style. The best surfers in the world heard about our South swell and came over and paddled out to surf with us. It was comical to watch them try to drop in and make that bottom turn; they were getting hammered, and it was super amusing for the locals.

The best surfers in the world were eating it, and the locals were killing it. Home turf surf, you bet, but finally some Hawaiians started figuring out our angle off-and-go technique. All you had to do was watch us because we were carving up waves, and they were getting smoked. That was another great summer day of surf in Coronado.

By then, the Marines were much cooler to surfers, but it was better to be with us because we had stars on our bumper, which meant an admiral's car. Everyone on the base knew what the stars represented, even if it was a car full of surfers.

SISTER SUE

The Ghetto was kept on an even keel because Sue Hacker lived there. She was like a big sister to all of us. Consequently, things were toned down quite a bit out of respect for her. When Sue graduated from San Diego State and moved to Idaho, things changed at the surf ghetto. First, there was room for one more surfer and secondly no one could keep us in check. All the surfers had girls coming over now. I'm sure they weren't telling their moms they were going to the Ghetto to party.

One of the guys who stayed in Sue's room for a while, Moe Eco, was the only part-time surfer who lived there besides Chip Lee, who had the other house. Surfers had two houses and the shack where I lived, and Chip had building number four. At first, we thought he was a cop, or a Narc, or something like that, but he did too many dumb things (maybe he was a flatfoot), like the time he ridiculed a guy at

Krishna Mulvaney's (restaurant and bar) for the way he drank a flaming hooker (Brandy in a shot glass set on fire). Chip wanted to show him how to do it and set his mustache on fire. I hate laughing at someone's misfortune, but Mr. Braggart got his dues. We didn't see him for a week and a half after that.

We surfed hard and partied hard all the time at the Ghetto, and we were known for being a lot of fun. The surfer compound had no supervision. We could be as wild as we wanted, and we liked it that way.

THE WHITE WHALE

Someone brought over this woman called The White Whale. She was a big wide girl, so not my type and she didn't go home like she was supposed to. I believe it was Timmy who dragged her over because she was in the Hacker house, where I had privileges (bathroom and kitchen), but I didn't hang out. When it came to girls, Timmy was much less discriminating than I was and I wasn't discriminating at all. Okay, I was. Still, the White Whale was not getting in the shack with a rack, but somehow, the crabs made it out there anyway (they were trying to get away, just like I was). The White Whale signaled me a few times, and I was like, no, no, no girl.

I just wanted to run, you know the little voice you hear that want to protect you? It was saying, "run for your life." That little voice was right about running because she brought crabs to the ghetto, and we all got them. I got them, and I couldn't even look at her because "not my type" was me being nice; she was way past that. We all got the special shampoo and we bombed the Hacker house and the shack, and that took care of it, but the damage was done to our sterling reputation because some girls must have gotten the crabs and taken them home to their families.

HUNGRY SURFER BOYS

Moe Eco's dad decided he wanted to cook for all the surfer boys, so about fifteen surfer boys showed up at the ghetto for the feast. He made the best lemon chicken and had a tasty Greek salad. Everything he brought was absolutely delicious; we ate and ate just because we could. Yes, in-shape surfers in their late teens and early 20s can eat a mountain of food and he knew it. Not only that, but he came and fed us twice. Yup, he came back for an encore. And I'm sure, just like me, all the surfer boys could have used a good meal. Thank you, Constance.

Since the Vietnam War was raging, our entire group of surfer boys was kind of eligible for the draft. Most of the ones older than me didn't even register; that way, they didn't have to dodge the draft. They all signed up after the war ended, and nobody seemed to care. Me, I was eighteen, the war machine didn't draft you until after your nineteenth birthday, and I was pretty sure they wouldn't take me after my trauma-filled childhood (Read *Hell House: True Stories from the Redheaded Stepchild*). I was dreaming. They were taking anyone they could; they needed bodies.

We, the surf ghetto's residents, decided to have a spaghetti dinner fundraiser for George McGovern. We made what we called Ghetto-Sketty. It was probably our best and biggest party too. We had plenty of girls, the usual ones plus some new ones too. After all, this was a political fundraiser; they weren't just going to the Ghetto to see handsome, studley, and wild surfer boys. We were respectable now (for some people in those days, surfers were synonymous with junkies) with our political fundraiser.

People who usually wouldn't be at our parties showed up. The rumors were true; we were fun guys and threw some awesome parties. Paul Acree showed up in a new yellow Pantera. I don't know what he was wrecked on, but he made an ass of himself and left. The debauchery continued, and soon a new, more respectable girl was in the shack. We had lots of girls coming over the Ghetto. We had local girls, Chula Vista girls, and girls from the Del Coronado on vacation; some of those girls returned every year.

BEBOP

BeBop was a cute little blondie who decided she was going to hang out at the Ghetto.

She liked all the guys who lived there (I never slept with her), and I think she was the sort of girlfriend of two different guys at different times. She was fun to be around but never came into the shack; that was a step too bold for her. BeBop was really good at being teased, which was good-hearted and ruthless at the same time because most of the surfer boys were pretty good guys, but we liked to play rough too. We kidded her a lot and she liked it, a true ghetto girl.

Her father was a high-ranking police officer in Coronado, and he had to know she was hanging out over at the Ghetto. A few times, her dad came by in his Coronado Police Lieutenant uniform to fetch her (when she was late for dinner or something), which was always interesting because the place tended to smell like marijuana. Her dad seemed like a nice man who refrained from judging us. Many other girls probably wanted to hang with all those Greek god-bodied surfers, but she was the only one brave enough to hobnob with us.

ENSENADA JAIL

One day, Big Al, I, and John Bomb decided to go surfing down at Three M's north of Ensenada, Baja California, Mexico. We had no problems getting there, but the conditions were incompatible with surfing when we got there. We set up camp at Three M's and decided to hang out in Ensenada for a while and see if things got a little better, even if we had to go north or south.

We knew most of the surf spots on Baja, especially the ones within a couple hundred miles of the border, but that's before we knew about Scorpion Bay.

We had a good lunch, with some cervezas in Ensenada and we were walking around the uptown part of what you would call the tourist area. It was around dusk when Big Al and John Bomb said they had to pee and walked into an alley to take care of that while I waited on the street. While I was standing there, I saw a shopkeeper come out of his shop, grab a police officer, and they approached Big Al and John Bomb when they came out of the alley. The shopkeeper told the policeman that they were peeing in the alley. They vehemently denied it, but the shopkeeper told the policeman where they peed in the alley, and the policeman showed them where they left their mark.

They should've just offered up the bribe, but they didn't, and a paddy wagon showed up, and they were going to jail. Lucky for me, I was not. I tried to reason with the police officer by asking him if we had to pay the fine at the police station or if we could pay it now, but he asked me if I wanted to go to jail, too. I told him I didn't, and Big Al threw me his keys to his VW truck.

So I got in Big Al's VW truck and was off to the Ensenada police station to find out what the bail was. That's when I found out something unique about Mexico and getting directions: Suppose you ask a Mexican for directions, and even if they don't know what you're talking about, they will point you in a direction so that they don't look stupid. The next thing you know, I had to ask people where Ensenada was...but I finally found the police station.

After waiting over an hour, they told me what the bail was. I was thinking twenty-four bucks each, but that was the street price they would've paid if they hadn't denied their urinating. Now I had to find the lockup where they were so I could try and get some money from them so I wouldn't have to drive back to Coronado to get the bail money. It was now dawn, and I had been up all night, and I had a feeling they'd been up all night, too. After arriving at the lockup, it took me about two hours to get some communication going to finish my task.

Lucky for all of us they had some money that John Bomb (who was a huge guy) had hidden in his sock. Then it was back to the police station to post their bail; once I did that, I went back to lockup with the paperwork to get them released. Even though it felt like forever, I'm sure it felt even longer for them.

I have never met two more grateful people than Big Al and John Bomb when I finally got them out of the Ensenada Jail. Boy, did they have some harrowing stories to tell. Here's Big Al's account of the inside of the Ensenada jail:

A small 10' by 10' room with people laid across the cement floor like sardines in a can. There was no available floor space. When the steel door slammed behind us, it got dark. With a little hallway light glistening through the barred opening in the door, I could see a small four-foot by two-foot ledge. It was the tail end of the one cement bench the head jail guard had commandeered for his bed.

I curled up at his feet. I hadn't been there but a minute when, out of nowhere, "WHAM!" My bunkmate kicked me in the head, and I fell onto a sleeping prisoner on the floor below me. He screamed in pain, and someone quickly screwed in the bare light bulb in the ceiling socket, and everyone stood up. I could now see there were about fifteen men, all Mexicans, and John and I – the only Gringos!

The man I rolled onto was standing right in front of me, his face streaming with blood. I had accidentally torn a large scab off the side of his face. Things were not looking good. He told me he also saw the gnarliest guy in there get handed an ice pick by one of the staff.

So, were they happy to see me? You bet! The jail was over a hundred years old and undoubtedly had some famous alumni. I heard it's a museum now, just like all the other notorious lockups that are museums today.

PAUL BRO

The Surf Ghetto was changing. Sue had graduated and was gone, Tim joined the Air Force, and Buddy had hitchhiked back east to his parent's house. One of the new inhabitants of the house was Paul Bro. He was a tortured soul, and things weren't going to get better anytime soon for him. I remember when I was in elementary school, we were told about this kid being punished in the summertime. We rode our bikes by his house on Eighth Street in the Country Club area, and sure enough, there he was, standing on a little cement square with the giant flagpole, and his nose was positioned to the flagpole, and he was standing at attention.

The flags were the US Stars and Stripes and the Marine Corps flag. That's the first time I'd seen Paul Bro. Apparently, he was there a lot; that's how we found out about his brutal punishment in the first place. Even then, as a child, I knew that was cruel and unusual punishment put on him by his psycho Marine daddy.

The following school year when I was walking home with my buddies Tombo and Kurt K, Paul came upon us as we were walking and asked us if we were looking for silver dollars. We looked at each other in acknowledgment that we had a real weirdo on our hands. Even at a young age, we knew there was something more than a little different about Paul. One time, we ended up throwing Paul's bike over a fence; I don't remember why, but when we all got in trouble we were kind of not allowed to hang out anymore.

But now it's years later, and Paul's living in the ghetto. That was an eye-opening experience. He was trying to be a Bro but was more like a "Sub-Bro." He was given the nickname Paul Bro, not because he was a bro, but quite the contrary, a mockingly or sarcastic type of serial maltreatment. Paul would never be a real Bro, but he was happy with his status in the group because he belonged as much as he ever had in his sad existence. He got made fun of a lot because it was easy, and he was asking for it. He was trying to surf, but was blind as a bat and couldn't surf without glasses. To prevent him from losing his glasses, he glued 76 Gas Station antenna balls to his glasses so they would float if he wiped out and lost them, all this after he had elaborately tied them to his head. He certainly looked different, with two orange balls fixed to each side of his head, out there with the other surfers, the real surfers, but he was trying!

He was a source of amusement for people he'd never met; some just wanted to get away from him, especially the girls. For someone who really didn't need anybody else picking on him, he set himself up constantly for the alternative (harassment and hazing). In living at the Ghetto, he had to enjoy the frat house-type initiation daily, gentle, loving torture.

One of the Bros came by every morning to catch him jacking off, and he would always take his blankets and throw them out the window. It was a daily ritual. The Bro Big Al would drive over every morning and sneak up on him, and then I'd hear the screaming; even if I was in the shack, I knew what had just happened, and it was every day, nonstop torture, pain and abuse.

There were plenty of girls around the Ghetto, but none for Paul.

NO MORE CHOWDER

Back at the Chowder House, things were getting stranger all the time. They showed zero respect to me and thought it was funny to mistreat me. Being a redhead, I was predisposed to that kind of treatment; everyone there thought it was okay to make a joke about me, my hair or the color of my skin and the clothes I wore. I was used to it. Here's a rhyme my favorite waitress made up; *Is Stu Stall stoned. Stu Stall sure still seems stoned.*

I was working at a place where I made no money and had no respect, and the owner was always letting me know she was after me or something, and it wasn't getting any better. She was my friend's mom. She already had six kids, and I was a teenager. The worst part of that summer was when they made some relative a waitress; she was absolutely horrible, probably the worst waitress ever. She was known as Princess Pure Bred. She and her family thought it was a compliment, an acknowledgment of their status. The person who gave her that nickname had a different opinion. He gave me this quote: "There's no lake, pond, river or stream shallower than Princess Pure Bred," and she wore that on her sleeve like a badge of honor. It was probably the first and last time she ever had to work. She proved every day that she didn't have the desire or the capacity and was always taking the other waitresses' orders because she couldn't wait for her customers' to come up, thereby screwing up the whole dining room.

Princess spent much of that summer belittling me and calling me names. I ignored her; I was building lots of character. But if I felt that I was being disrespected before she arrived, it reached new heights with this spoiled prima donna. I knew it was time for me to leave. Actually, I knew it was time for me to leave on the first day I worked there. Now it was way past time to leave. I was growing up fast and needed out of there.

One night, I was partying when the Chowder House owner and her sidekick, Missy Why, found me and hustled me into some guy's van. Then they took me to Tijuana, where we all drank. On the way home, my friend's mom was all over me; I was getting grossed out. Even though I was drunk, I wasn't into it. I had nowhere to run. I thought about opening the van door and rolling onto the Silver Strand. Still, I knew that would not be without injuries, but the thought kept creeping into my mind. Finally, we were back in Coronado, and I was able to get out of the back of that van and run.

Having your friend's drunk mom hit on you is a spine-chilling experience, but it wasn't as bad as the woman who lived next door to her. She was always after me too, and once she trapped me in her bedroom when I was collecting for my paper route, and she wanted to "show me her house." I'm pretty sure she wanted to show me more than that. Maybe she was skillful, but I didn't want to find out. It was always a tense situation when I ran into her. She was always after me and never gave it a break. She was less than half a block away when I lived in the beach cottage and half a block from the Chowder House, so I always saw her. She gave up about ten years later, and she would always let me know by being over the top, totally indifferent, like an insolent teenager. She was still over twice my age. I knew I needed to change my life, and getting away from the people preying on me was an excellent way to start.

KRISHNA MULVANEY'S

There was a new restaurant in the old Tradewinds which was an old Seal UDT bar. One morning, on my paper route riding down Orange Avenue, I was passing by the Tradewinds when I heard the door opening and they threw some guy out. It was maybe 5:15 AM. Then, I heard the door open again, and they threw another guy out.

That's about all I knew about Tradewinds, and now it was becoming Krishna Mulvaney's and I wanted out of the Chowder House. They hired me to do kitchen work prep, like preparing crab legs and making chowder and salad, with the promise that in time they would teach me how to be a broiler man. That sounded great, but I soon realized I wanted to be out of the kitchen too. They had two busboys the first night, but they brought me in as the third busboy because they knew they would be busy; everyone was a rookie and needed help on the floor.

The manager didn't like my long curly dark red hair, (lots of girls did though) as he was a real square jock type, which explains why the other two guys they hired for busboys were also lame.. The manager didn't want me on the floor because I had long curly red hair down to my ass when it was wet and to the middle of my back when it was dry and curled up. He was a strait-laced jock from that era where they drank a lot and hated people who smoked weed. I did ten times as much work as the two of them put together, but the next day, I was back in the kitchen. That didn't last long. The waiters wanted the other two guys gone with me in their place. It was a good deal for management, too. I could do ten times more work so, for now, I was a busboy and a prep guy.

The Mulvaney's people hired two girls from Imperial Beach—Linda and Sandy, a blonde and a brunette—to be cocktail waitresses. We instantly hit it off, even though they were both older than me. Linda and Sandy loved my hair and they instantly captivated me with their beauty. They knew I was poor, and one of the waiters who was in my Boy Scout troop told them about my mother's devastating death. They were sweet and gorgeous, and I still love them to this day.

One day I showed up and Sandy had a bunch of Hawaiian shirts as a gift for me. A few days later, she asked me if she could take care of me. Yeah, I was stupid and naïve and eighteen, so I didn't really get it, but I could have been living with a beautiful woman, and she would have kept me out of trouble too. Almost like déjà vu as I'm sure other beautiful women would have keep me out of trouble as well.

After a few months of bussing tables, the manager came to me and said,

"If you cut your hair, I'll make you a waiter."

I would have been the only underage waiter in the company, but I was obstinate and didn't think it was fitting that he held that over my head.

GOING, GOING, GONE

All good things must end, and with Luki Pooler's death, the Ghetto was about to be bulldozed. It was the first of many new projects that would eventually change Coronado from a quiet little village into an overcrowded, traffic-congested suburb of San Diego. Once we got notice, I got an alley house with Goob, a two bedroom one bath with a one-car garage, a front yard on the alley, and a side yard about five blocks from the beach, all for a hundred eighty-five dollars a month.

Wow. I was living in a real house for the first time in a while, and it had everything. Timmy Hacker had joined the Air Force, Desperate got his own home and Chip Lee disappeared. We always thought Chip was a cop or a Narc; he probably returned to his police unit and we never saw him again. The new house was cool, but it wasn't the same. The surf ghetto had girls who just showed up randomly, but things were a little calmer at the new house, and I was nineteen now. Most of the surfer boys, including me, were still in party mode while I lived in the alley house, and we had a few great parties.

Jimmy and I started sweeping girls off their feet by taking them skinny dipping at some of the local pools. The first time, we had three girls in my Saab, and we hit the Del pool until security ran us off naked. Then we hit the Glorietta Bay Hotel, right across the street, and finally, we hit the Coronado Shores pool on the ocean. This became a regular thing after parties. We even had girls coming up to us and asking if they could go. The hotels were onto us, so we made a list of apartments with pools in the front, close to the street, and we started hitting them.

Still, we didn't stay long because we weren't even trying to be quiet. I'm sure we woke lots of people up, but it was probably the most fun anyone ever had in those pools. The best part was driving around town with naked girls in the car. God that was fun. I think the last time we did it, we only had one girl, but it was Nancy, so it was okay. We ran from the Shores when the rent-a-cop expected us to stay for the police. Yeah right! We jumped over the wall naked and ran to my car.

Most of the surfer boys went into the construction business as laborers and carpenters. Not me. I knew I had a brain and wanted to use it to make my daily bread instead of beating up my body to make a living. I moved from the Chowder House and now worked at Krishna Mulvaney's. I tried attending junior college at Sweetwater (too far) and Mesa College (which looked like Coronado High School). I didn't make it through the semester at either. I just wasn't ready. Too much stuff was happening in my life, and not all of it was good.

THE MONGOOSE

The surfer boys hung out at Center Beach when they weren't surfing. One of the boy's dads talked the city into letting him rent inner tubes, boogie boards, surfboards, surf rafts, and that kind of stuff out of a little trailer that he towed down the beach in the morning and picked up every evening. We were are all down there getting copious amounts of future skin cancer as none of us wore any sunscreen, hats, or any protection of any kind. We all loved the beach life, surfing, sun, and girls, along with going on four or five-hour surf trips all over the coast up to Doheny State Beach and down past Ensenada in Baja California. We were an instant crowd because all of us were in fantastic shape. We were good surfers, and we came to get waves.

    There was this Chula Vista girl my surfer Bros knew was after me, and she wasn't bashful about it, like me, her prey. I knew it too, and I found her very interesting even though

I'd never spoken to her. My surfer Bros were so confident that we'd get together that they gave her a nickname before we knew her real name. They called her "The Mongoose."

She was a tall girl, but I could see she had a Playboy bunny body from her bathing suit. She drove around Coronado in this big yacht-sized blue Lincoln Continental. It was huge, but a big girl needs a big car—which is something she told me that after we got acquainted. She got that line from her dad when he gave her the car. She wasn't shy about her desire for me, and I planned on making it easy for her. The beach thing went on for a while, and she had her blonde girlfriend with her constantly; they were part of a larger Chula Vista gang of girls on the prowl for boys in Coronado.

I'd finally gotten a new used car, a little blue Saab. I liked it a lot, and one day I was out doobie cruising with one of my surfer Bros (smoking a joint driving around town). We saw The Mongoose and her blonde girlfriend cursing the big blue Lincoln Continental. The next thing you know, she was getting pulled over by the police, so I put the doobie out, rolled down the windows all the way, and pulled up behind the cops. It was the nice cop that I knew from my paper route, Officer McCool. By now, my surfer Bro, Baby, who I was smoking weed with (he got that nickname for being the most spoiled brat ever in Coronado, and that's saying something in a town full of spoiled brats) was starting to get nervous. I told him,

"Be cool, I know the cop."

So Jerry McCool approaches my car and says, "Stuart, what are you doing?"

But because Baby is starting to melt down again, I had to tell him, "Be cool, come on man, I know what I'm doing."

I told McCool, "I want to rescue those girls."

"Stuart, stay right here and don't move." Baby's now starting to act like itchy brother, but I was amused watching the entitled mama's boy squirm (he never even thanked me for what I was about to do for him). We watched the cops put both girls through the road drunk driving test, walking the line and all that stuff. Then Jerry returns to the car and says, "They're kind of borderline. I gave them a choice: they can either come with us down the station, and we will call their parents to pick them up, or they can go with you guys, but that car can't move until morning."

I said, "We'll take them."

And Jerry left to get them, and he brought them back to my car. As they walked up, I told Baby: "You need to get in the back with yours."

So, both girls got in the car. The Mongoose was sitting shotgun. I drove right over to Baby's house and kicked the two in the backseat out. That was a surprise to everyone, but me and you should have seen the look on the other girl's face. The Mongoose wasn't bothered by any of that. She looked at me and said, "I like your style."

"Yeah, I like your style too, girl. We're going to have a good time."

Then I took The Mongoose to my house and right into the bedroom—none of this living room chit-chat with this girl. I must say she was very accommodating and experienced. After an hour we took a break, and I heard a beer can opening. She had a Burgie tallboy and offered me one. I didn't want one, but I accepted it to be polite. She took me by surprise, and because she offered it and I didn't want to offend, I reluctantly started trying to drink my not-too-cold Burgie tallboy.

I had difficulty choking down that warm Burgie, but she immediately polished off her tallboy and went for another one. Somehow, she smuggled three tall boys in her purse out of that car with the cops right there after she'd just finished the field test for drunk driving (I was impressed. My kind of girl!).

Here I was, sitting in my bed with a naked teenager, sporting a *Playboy* centerfold body (okay, maybe *Hustler*) and I was drinking a lukewarm Burgie Tallboy.

I wanted more sex, as she was very talented in that regard. Instead, I'm choking down a warm beer I shouldn't have accepted in the first place because she wanted that one for herself. I had only choked down half of my Burgee by the time she drank two, but I must admit I had a newfound admiration for her. I asked her if she wanted to finish mine, and she did. I thought, alright, we can return to our action-packed night.

In the morning, I asked The Mongoose if she wanted me to pick up her friend before I took her to her car. She said: "Fuck Nancy" and she did. I heard that Nancy had to call her mom to come get her. Nancy was a pretty girl, and I dated her sister a few years later. I took her to the Richard Pryor show at the Golden Hall, where we were the only Caucasian couple there. She let me know how uncomfortable that made her right after the show. That comment made me think about making her mom come get her as well, but I'm not that kind of guy. Well, I never got her in my bed, but a few months later I came home and Jimmy Riley had her in my bed. Sometimes, it's all about timing. I guess mine was never in sync with hers.

The Mongoose didn't fit my normal profile, but there was something very attractive about her, and it wasn't just the *Playboy* bunny body. Her wit was off the charts. She had a quick mouth and took it to the edge of being mean, but she wasn't. She was super sarcastic, though, and I liked the challenge. She certainly got an extra helping of sassy, that's for sure, and she was exceptionally athletic and strong. The sweetness was hidden, but I swear it was there concealed somewhere in her brassiness.

She was sassy, not to be confused with bitchy, because she wasn't. My affair with the Mongoose was a lot of fun. Every time I got her in bed, it was always with Burgie tallboys. Yeah, even though I was a teenager and hadn't had a lot of relationships, I knew that was kind of strange; it was funny at first but got old sort of quickly. It was the Burgies and "a what's wrong with this picture" moment, and I stopped calling her, but here I am fifty years later, and I'd like to see her because she was a lot of fun and I've laughed my way through this story. I hope the big girl didn't get too big and stopped drinking, but I'll bet she's still fun no matter what.

About a dozen years later, I ran into the Mongoose (aka Linda) uptown in Coronado. It was about eleven thirty in the morning on a weekday. I could tell she'd been drinking, and she was instantly all over me. She was still super sexy, and that mouth was still running sassy. I liked it. I wanted her. She was a lot of fun, but she was trying to have sex with me up against my car on the side street off Orange.

At the same time, her girlfriend just stood there and watched (by now, lots of other people were watching, too). She was a walking spectacle, and I definitely wanted to have sex with her, but not in public. I tried talking her into going to my house. She seemed super-hot to get going, but no, she wanted to go to the bar. So, I went with her and her friend into Mulvaney's. However, I still had visions of getting her over to my house as her drunken ass and outright sexiness was making me horny. She was still the epitome of sexy and sultry.

After she had a few drinks and I had none, we left the place with her friend still tagging along. Now we're back against my car (literally) and she was all over me again. Yes, it was an actual exhibition, and the same people came out to watch again, but it wasn't bothering me. I was really horny now, and I was about to acquiesce, but now she wanted to go back to the bar. I walked with her when she said, "We're like Mutt and Jeff and you're Mutt." (she always pushes it right to the edge).

She is about 6'1" and had on 6-inch heels. She towered over me and I'm certainly not short. I laughed because it was funny, but I only had one thing on my mind: getting over to my house and getting her naked. Apparently, she wasn't into that and just wanted to do me on the side street. By now, plenty of people were watching from a distance, and I knew it was time for me to go on without her.

I ran into her at Mulvaney's the following New Year's Eve. She was wrecked, not just on booze, but she told me she'd been using Crystal, tweak or something. I wasn't paying attention; I had other things on my mind, but this time I got her over to my house, but unfortunately for me I never got her clothes off. She was still fun with that wicked mouth, and I remember it being wicked in more ways than one. I did have a good time partying with her, but I really wanted to have sex with her.

It made me wish I had some Burgie tallboys. I'd throw them in the bed and tell her to get them. That's when she told me she was married. I'm thinking, what, at four o'clock in the morning, what's this married shit, and what are you doing here anyway? She left before the sun came up and I was glad to see her go, kind of. The crystal made her not as much fun; it wasn't just that she didn't get naked; that shit steals something from you. I liked her but haven't seen her since, but I'm still laughing about her.

THE DARK SIDE RISES

Next door to Jimmy's parent's home, in the alley, was another Navy family with a son named CJ. He and Jimmy had become friends, sort of, and through Jimmy I became familiar with CJ too. CJ was going to Cal Western College in Point Loma. It was a wild school then, with lots of surfers and weed. He was a pot smoker, just like the rest of us. Apparently, CJ had a lot of connections in the marijuana business. Not only was Coronado full of smugglers, but evidently Point Loma was too. Later in my career, I found out that everyone in Santa Cruz was a drug dealer. I got to go with CJ and Jimmy to Cal Western. It was kind of a strange place. Some weird buildings I found out later were built by a woman trying to create a utopian society based on music and dance. Apparently, she was quite wealthy, which helped her build these architecturally curious buildings.

The drug trade at Cal Western was flourishing, and a big company worked out of there and other places in Point Loma. Then they all got busted and it was a big bust, but CJ somehow escaped, maybe because he was involved with distribution.

I love my surfer Bros, but when I needed a little more intellectual stimulation, I would go hang out with my old pal Albert Earl Sweeney, aka Big Al. We've been close friends since nursery school, crown elementary school, and the Episcopal Church. His dad, a Navy pilot, died when he was in first or second grade, and his mom married another Navy guy who had seven kids. She already had five, but they had one more to seal the deal. They had this huge house on Sixth and A, and Big Al had control of part of the basement, where he made T-shirts and all kinds of other stuff like driver's licenses.

At first, he was working with black and white licenses, and all he did was turn your picture around so he didn't have a profile. All profiles were for people under twenty-one, so they never even had to check your birthdates if you had a profile instead of a regular headshot. Now, Al was making the new colored licenses and working on them every time I went there. We'd smoke weed and watch *Star Trek*; I never watched *Star Trek* at my house, but I saw all the episodes at least twice in Big Al's basement.

One day I went over there and he showed me a thirty-three times magnifier. Then he showed me a driver's license that he had pulled apart. With his thirty times magnifier, he found the bubble wrap manufacturer on top of the original colored California State driver's license. A couple of weeks later he called me and invited me over to show me the mini bubble wrap he purchased directly from the manufacturer. Then he told me he only had one problem now. He needed all the forms the DMV used to make the licenses and couldn't figure out how to get them.

I said, "I know where you can get them."

"Where?"

"The DMV," I said with a big smile on my face,

Al said, "Well, sure, but they're not going to just hand them to you."

"If you play your cards right, they will just hand them to you." That interested him.

"How is that?"

I replied, "When you go in to get your driver's license, you take the test, and if you pass, they hand you a clipboard to take over to where you get your picture taken, and on that clipboard are all the forms you would ever need. (Some big wig thought having the clients carry the water (forms) was smart, until it wasn't.) Then, you walk right out the door with all the forms that you will ever need and they'll never even know you were there."

Al said, "No way,"

I said, "You've been there, think about it. That's what they do."

About ten days later he called me and said he took CP, the admiral's daughter, to the DMV. She walked out with every form he would ever need to forge California State licenses.

Then he said, "I always thought I was a lot smarter than you,"

I said, "I appreciate that, Bro."

One afternoon, CJ came to me. He said he had a Hawaiian friend coming in with a bale of really good weed. He needed a place to clean it up and get it ready for sale. He asked if he could do this work at my house that I rented with Goob. Goob was okay with it, so we invited some of the Bros over, who wanted to enjoy some good stinky and sticky Hawaiian buds.

The bale showed up with a guy by the name of Glen K who was with Clancy. The bale looked big at first, but it just kept expanding, and pretty soon it filled the entire living room, and our living room was quite large. So, we invited the other surfer Bros over and soon we were smoking great Hawaiian weed and cleaning up the buds. It was like a party where we got to work, and our pay was excellent weed. It took us two or three hours. It was a lot of work but fun. We all got nice bags of weed out of it, and Glen just kept rolling joints. We all got super stoned. Now, nobody in Coronado had better weed than the surfer boys.

Glenn was a cool guy. His dad was a famous lifeguard at Waikiki and best friends with the Duke. Glenn seemed to like me and was grateful for allowing him to use our space. He told me when I got to Hawaii to look him up. He knew I'd be coming for the huge surf someday.

A few days later, I was at the beach checking out the surf when Eddie Otero pulled up in a Porsche, which he bought for his girlfriend (or maybe it was his girlfriend's Porsche). He was dating an older woman who was my babysitter when I was a kid until my mom caught her on the couch with her boyfriend. I knew Eddie stopped to chat me up. He pulled out a joint and wanted to smoke it with me. I smoked it with him, then I pulled out a Hawaiian doobie, and fired that baby up.

He was blown away. I don't think Eddie had ever smoked weed that good. Ed asked me where I got it. I said from a Hawaiian guy. A few days later, Eddie stopped by my house and tried to recruit me into smuggling weed with him and Bob Lahodny. Eddie had been kicked out of the Coronado Company because they didn't like splitting profits four ways when they could split three ways. The company started as just Eddie and Paul Acree, and they added Lance because they couldn't afford to pay him, and it was easier to make him a partner.

Lance was the guy who knew how to smuggle and all the little nuances that went along with the trade. The company had a new boss, Lou Villar, who was initially hired to translate. The job that Eddie and Paul Acree did became redundant; one of them had to go. I turned down his offer and was happy that I did because I heard later that on their first job Bob got a rope wrapped around his neck when they were launching from Mexico. Eddie dragged him through the surf while piloting a zodiac inflatable boat for about a hundred and fifty yards.

PARTY TIME

It was always party time in Coronado when I was a teenager. It wasn't just the teenagers but all the adults, too. One of the surfers in the Bros was an offspring of robber barons, maybe more than one. The family had a ranch in the backwoods of San Diego County. The property had three houses, two little ones, and a big one with a pool. It was decided that all the Bros would go up there and party. A keg was bought, and we drank and drank and drank. We were even encouraged to drink in the morning when we woke up. I was never a big drinker, except the few times when I got really drunk as a teenager. I mean falling and puking drunk, but I became pragmatic before I knew that word.

The same robber baron's offspring had a father divorced from his mother, and he owned one-third of a house in *La misión* in Baja California. The other thirds were owner by

Bill Nye, head of the finance department at San Diego State with a PhD from Wharton, and Judge Vaughn, the head judge of the Juvenile Court. I got to know them all. We would go down to Mexico and get drunk. The two parties I went to on the outskirts of San Diego were boring (no girls). It was just drinking, and I only went to parties to dance with girls. It was most of the surfer boys out there and some of the female offspring of the robber barons. The *La misión* house attracted more girls for some reason (it was BYOG).

I liked going to Mexico in those days. I found the Mexican people very friendly, especially the poor Mexicans. When I was a kid, our parents took the whole family to Ensenada. My mother and father had some attachment to Ensenada; I believe it was a romantic attachment. On our way home, our car broke down, and a poor Mexican family took us in. They fed us, allowed us to rest, and somehow got the family to the border. My dad came back and got the car later in the week.

I probably went on over a hundred surf trips to Mexico, from days to week-long camping trips. I loved Baja in those days, but these days, you can't do any of that kind of stuff. It's either not allowed, doesn't happen anymore, or it's too dangerous. It's changed so much. I raised two boys in Coronado, about ten miles from the Mexican border, and I never took them to Mexico. It's just too risky.

PARTY TIME

I was partying with the surfer boys and girls at *La misión* when we decided to go to La Fonda, a Mexican bar, restaurant, and hotel. It was a fun place, with Mariachis and dancing. I was there about fifteen minutes when I ran into this beautiful girl I'd been chatting with in Coronado at Mulvaney's. Her name was Demi. Her parents would come down to Coronado on the weekends from Los Angeles, and they liked Mulvaney's. I really liked her. She was super nice, smart and gorgeous. We had some interesting conversations.

And now I was hanging out with her at La Fonda. She was a lot of fun to be around. We talked for over an hour when the group said, "It's time to go." I asked her if she wanted to return to *La misión* with us, and she said "yes." We all got loaded up in the car and were about ready to take off when her stepfather came out and retrieved her. If he had come a minute later, we would have been returning to *La misión* and were not coming back till the morning.

I was despondent, and when I got back to the house, I drank about half a bottle of tequila. Then I went down to the beach to puke. I'd undoubtedly drunk more than I could handle, and I was down there barfing when a couple of guys jumped me. They had me pinned down as I was unable to fight back due to being too drunk, and I heard one of them say, "It's Stuart Stall."

It was Coronado guys and they were smuggling weed for the company.

I learned later that Lou Villar, who at the time had the most southern house in *La misión*. I acquired that knowledge from Paul Acree, "the rat," one day while he and I were driving to Punta Colonet to make a connection with the Mexican provider of kilos (2.2 pounds of marijuana pressed into bricks). A week later, we went down by the sea and shot off two flares so our connection would know we could make it there and back.

The Coronado guys who were holding me down got permission to let me go because the cops would be all over the place if I didn't get back to the house. I was pretty hung over the next day, and I'll bet they were pretty surprised to find me relaxing on the beach, but it now makes a good story.

About a week later, I got a call from an irate man who turned out to be Demi's stepfather. He was very threatening and accused me of being with an underage girl. I told him I never even tried to kiss her, and that didn't seem to do anything to satisfy his rage. He kept after me and started mentioning Mulvaney's in Coronado, too, which means they made her confess, and they had to know nothing happened. I told him all we did was talk in the United States and Mexico when he accused me of kidnapping her. He kept saying underage again and a bunch of other crap too. I'd had enough of him, so I told him, "I think they have different laws in Mexico as far as that goes." Then I hung up on him and never heard from him again.

When I started writing this, I looked up her age and couldn't believe she was that much younger than me, but all we ever did was talk. At least for me, things can become slightly confusing when I get around someone as beautiful as her. Her stepdad was right, but I'm pretty sure she was the original instigator.

The next time I saw Demi, I was the *Maitre d'* and waiting tables at the Chez when she came in with her husband. The hostess that night said she was the new girl on some soap opera. She was pretty happy to see me, and I was happy to see her, too. I hadn't seen her in a few years, but her husband was not pleased to see her being happy to see me. It was almost like he didn't fit into our conversation. Apparently, he was the front man for some band I've never heard of. He paid with his credit card, and I saw his last name was Moore. He didn't leave a decent tip, but I'm okay with that. I got to see that beautiful woman again that I had some strange connection to and hadn't seen for a few years, so the tip was undoubtedly an afterthought.

The next time I saw her was about eight years later at the Coronado Brigantine. She was sitting alone at the bar, and they cleared space around her because her presence was too intimidating for anyone except me to sit next to her. I pulled up beside her and asked, "How's it going?"

"Hi Stuart. It's Stuart, right?"

We had a lovely conversation until she said, "I've got to get back to the Hotel Del Coronado."

"You're taking me with you, aren't you?"

She laughed. "I would if I didn't have my husband with me."

I don't know if that was true or if she was trying to be nice. Anyway, it was a good night for me. I'd like to say that's another beautiful woman I wanted and who I let get away, but I was probably just dreaming.

GARAGE SAILING

Garage sales in Coronado were semi-famous around San Diego. Many people from all over the county would cross the bridge or ferry over in the good old days.

Coronado garage sales had a lot of treasures, the stuff navy guys brought home from all over the world. There were antiques from the east coast and trinkets from all over the planet. My old boss from the Chowder House was still after me and asked me if I wanted to go to some garage sales with her on Thursday (the day the local paper came out; all the garage sales were in the classified section). At that point, I didn't know how to say no to her, so I agreed.

She showed up at my house at seven forty-five in the morning, came right in the front door and into my bedroom, and jumped in bed with me. I ran out the other side, grabbed my pants, and scooted into the bathroom. I wasn't interested. One other time I woke up with her sucking on my fingers. I found that revolting. None of my other friend's moms were trying to jump me, but her redheaded neighbor was always trying to lure me into her home. She was on my old paper route and took me on a tour of her house when I was collecting for the paper. I barely got out of there. She had me, her fifteen year-old paper boy trapped in her bedroom, but I escaped, so now I was always wary of her.

Not my type, to say the least. Plus I had to deal with the gay couple that lived on my paper route. The husband had his secret boyfriend, and the wife had her secret girlfriend. It was all secret, except that it wasn't. They were known as fine, upstanding citizens when they were in each other's beds. They even had four kids. Sometimes it was a strange little town, all kinds of people living double lives and acting rich when most of the town was poor. Coronado was known for cheap rent and a place for big families. However, that started to change when the bridge to San Diego opened, and they got rid of the beautiful ferries.

IT'S GETTING DARK

My time at that cute and super functional alley house was over. The landlord's daughter was moving in, and Goob was moving to Colorado with his girlfriend, so I moved in with CJ. I was still working as a busboy at Mulvaney's. I was an ardent little saver with some money to invest. CJ didn't have a job. He had a business, a marijuana business. He had an open room because the guy in that room, Bobby H, had gotten busted with some weed somewhere.

Bobby was now on his way to South America with a hollow surfboard, and he was looking to score some nice llama blankets and some pure evil white powder (aka cocaine). Soon, I was investing in CJ's enterprise, and Jimmy became involved too. He had connections. His youngest sister, five years older than him, had an involved boyfriend; his brother was also involved. That brother had a girlfriend four years older than me, but I had a crush on her since I first saw her, Betsy B. She was a beautiful woman and she seemed to like me too.

All these people had strong connections that allowed us to do marijuana arbitrage with people we knew in Coronado who were smuggling and people in North County and elsewhere. CJ had inherited two really good connections for distribution: One was Little Jimmy, but we called him "Little Ricky," because we thought he looked like a little Ricky Ricardo and the other one was a group of guys up in Washington state. We had a guy in Coronado who loved driving weed and had his sidekick, Hammer, along for the ride. He was investing too, so we had a little group of people who invested with us.

One day, CJ brought a black guy over to the house and then one of the Washington guys arrived. CJ had met the guy at Cal Western and he had some art and gold coins to sell that he got from someone's home. The Washington guy bought the art, and CJ purchased the coins. Then the guy wanted to gamble and play craps with dice and a blanket. That's where I came in and won some money in the craps game.

Then CJ told the guy from Cal Western I could do thirty push-ups in thirty seconds. The guy said bullshit and we had a bet. I got Elizabeth, CJ's wife, out of the house to write down all the bets. Then I asked anyone (including some surfers who showed up and the Washington guy) if anyone wanted to get in at thirty-five, and almost everyone did except my surfer Bros and CJ. After that, there was a discussion about what my push-up would look like. I told them,

"My back will be straight the entire time, my chest will touch the ground every time, and my arms will be fully extended when I go up."

Then the black guy said, "I want to put my hand under your chest to make sure you touch."

I told him, "I will smash your hand."

He said, "I don't care."

And I asked "Anyone want to make a side bet that he can't keep his hand down?" That got some chuckles but no bets, so I said, "Who wants to get in at forty?"

That surprised many people (including me), and they all bet. Even Jimmy Reilly bet against me and the surfers who'd all seen me do thirty plenty of times, but not CJ. He said, "I want in at fifty,"

I quickly replied, "Deal, but just you."

It was time to perform. I knew I had to go hard, and that I was going to hurt the next day, and maybe I was a little hesitant letting CJ in at fifty, I'd never let anyone bet fifty before. A surfer named Pat had the stopwatch, the black guy put his hand down, and I was off.

He might have lasted five pushups because I was literally bouncing off the ground, except when his hand was down, I had an inch less to go. All I was doing was pushing up and dropping, but no one could see that because I was going so fast. I stopped at fifty-four push-ups with four seconds left to go. It was a good day, but the next day, I really hurt.

Bobby returned from Peru with his gorgeous Llama blanket and all the other stuff he successfully brought into the country. Then he was gone again to the East Coast. I got talked into visiting little Ricky in Bangor, Maine. I was flying with two suitcases that probably weighed over forty pounds each as I was carrying a little over seventy-five pounds of marijuana in the suitcases. To finish getting ready for the job, I cut off all my long, beautiful, curly red hair, to the chagrin of many female admirers who just loved it. I didn't even know until they told me, but they sure made their feelings about my haircut known.

I went to Jimmy Riley's house, and he cut off all my hair. We put it in a brown paper bag and stuffed it in the Eugenia bush on his patio. I walked into work at Mulvaney's that evening. It was a Friday night, and they had never seen me with short hair. The manager looked at me and said, "So you want to be a waiter?"

I said, "That would be nice."

He immediately called over one of the waiters working that night, fired him on the spot, and gave me his shift. To say I was surprised was an understatement, and Bucky never forgave me for the firing and harasses me to this day.

Kind of like one of my surfer Bro's wives who threw herself at me when she first came to town, and I wasn't interested at all.

Now, I was a waiter at Mulvaney's, the only under-twenty-one-year-old waiter in the company. I was making more money now, allowing me to put more money into the business. I asked for a couple of days off work from Mulvaney's to visit Little Ricky with my two suitcases. I wrapped the kilos in plastic and put some clothes around the outside of them; the two suitcases were stuffed and heavy. I got dropped off at Lindbergh Field, walked up to the counter of Delta Air Lines, where I'd made a phone reservation with a fake name, and bought my ticket with cash, using my alias.

The ticket agent picked up my bags and said, "Wow, these are kind of heavy."

I replied: "Yeah, they're filled with a lot of books. I'm on my way back to college."

In those days, they didn't care about cash payments and never checked your ID. Plus, books and kilos had the same shape. It was a long flight to Bangor, Maine, through Dallas, Atlanta, Baltimore, Boston, and finally Bangor. They served the same breakfast after every stop, and I ate them all, but I was in good shape and didn't want to cause any disturbance.

That supposedly was the safest way to go, and it worked for me. Little Ricky picked me up, and we drove south to his hometown, Fall River, Massachusetts. The place looked like it had been condemned during the Depression, and I felt an eerie sadness come over me as we drove around.

He told me these were working factories that I thought were condemned in the Depression, but Little Ricky said people were working in them every day. Wow, that was sad and heartbreaking. I'd never seen anything like that before. Little Ricky took my load of weed somewhere, then returned, and we went out to party at the Pink Elephant nightclub. I had girls coming to me; right away one of them told me she liked my tan. I don't remember anyone ever saying that to this red-skinned, redheaded, freckled face surfer. I never had a tan. I just got red…and even redder when I felt uncomfortable.

She asked me what I did for a living, and I told her I was a pot smuggler. She laughed and asked me what I really did, and I told her I was an insurance agent. For some reason, she liked that better than the truth. The following day, Little Ricky dropped me off at the Providence, Rhode Island airport, and I flew back to LAX and then back to Lindbergh Field. I got the cash later, but it went through CJ, so I didn't get all the cash I should have.

A few weeks later, I did it again, and this time, I came home with a couple of pounds of Red Colombian I got from

Little Ricky. A lot of people to this day tell me it was the best weed they'd ever smoked. It was a little seedy, but I saved all those seeds and gave them to CJ later that year. He took them to Hawaii, where another surfer grew unbelievably good marijuana in that iron oxide rich soil on Kauai.

YOU CAN BANK ON THAT

One day our driver, Cool Breeze, got a call from a local guy who was a favorite son sailor and big shot at the Coronado Yacht Club, saying he needed someone to drive a large boat to the East Coast for a sailboat race. The boat belonged to the president and CEO of Home Federal Savings and Loan, last name of Fletcher.

We said yes because it was a golden opportunity to stuff that boat full of weed and send it to the east coast. Hello, Little Ricky. We laughed and laughed and laughed about all the famous San Diego family who was now supporting our business of realizing the American dream.

Our driver set off towing the first of three boats packed full of weed. They always took Route 20, as that was the safest route, but had a mishap in Kansas City, where the Fletcher's station wagon used to tow the boat was wrecked. When the drivers reported the wreckage back to the famous sailor, he reported it to the Fletchers, but the only thing they were worried about was the boat full of weed (they didn't know about the weed). We were concerned about it, too, but for different reasons. We didn't want anyone to get busted or lose our load. And the Fletcher family could have cared less about the car. They only cared about the boat, and soon Cool Breeze and Hammer had a nice truck to pull that boat with and they were off to Virginia where they were supposed to deliver the boat. But first, Cool Breeze and Hammer had to get the boat full of weed to Fall River, Massachusetts, to unload our cargo. It was another successful trip despite the accident.

Cool Breeze and Hammer also got a scare in Oklahoma when they stopped for gas and drinks. A trooper followed them into the mini-mart and said, "You boys wouldn't have that boat full of marijuana, would you?"

Cool Breeze, who wasn't feeling too cool right then, said, "No Sir, we're driving that boat to the East Coast for a banker so he can be in a sailboat race." The trooper squinted his eyes, gave them the stare, then nodded and moved on.

We were doing pretty well with our loads to Washington and the East Coast with Little Ricky and the Washington guys. Still, our regular driver decided he was done, so my buddies Jimmy and Bobby, who was back from South America and the East Coast, decided to take a load to little Ricky. Bobby wanted to get back to the East Coast anyway, so they got a drive away from either Hertz or Avis, I forget which one. The rental car companies would pay you a nominal fee to drive a car from coast to coast; it was a nice tool for smugglers. Off they went, but we found out a couple of days later they'd been busted in El Paso because they took Route 10 instead of Route 20 and got caught at a border checkpoint outside of El Paso.

It was hard to believe someone was so stupid as to take the 10, not the 20, and go through another border checkpoint that could have been completely avoided. I lost a lot of money, but the worst part was that my best friend got busted, and I felt sad about that. Soon, he was out of jail. His parents bailed him out and got him a good lawyer named Philip DeMassa. I don't know how it turned out for Bobby (I haven't seen him since), but Jimmy got off somehow. I should have taken that as a sign to get out of the business, but I didn't. We got our regular drivers, Cool Breeze and Hammer, back and did a few more loads to Washington and we recouped most of our money, but things were changing.

CJ had made a deal that I'm not sure what the details were, but he sent some kilos to the East Coast to little Ricky that were fronted to him by the Coronado Company. I wasn't there, but I heard Eddie Otero came over to the house and had a fistfight with CJ. I don't know what the argument was about, but Eddie was a thick bully type, and

CJ was small and wiry. I got the blow-by-blow account that sounded like CJ landed more punches than Eddie. Still, somehow, they ended up getting little Ricky's contact information, and they stole the connection. that was something the company never had before, good distribution, and Little Ricky could move a lot of weed.

That prompted CJ to think about moving to the Hawaiian Island of Kauai. When he went there to scout things out, his little wife threw herself at me, but I wasn't interested. Actually, I was, but I'm not the kind of guy that screws my friend's wives (although I've been offered the opportunity plenty of times). And she wasn't the first or last one to do that, but I never went for it. A couple of days later, Bob Lahodny came to the house and took her somewhere; he was a known screwer of his friend's wives. I don't know what they did to CJ or what transpired, but he was done. They moved to Hawaii.

M

I loved my little blue Saab. It was a great car. I didn't really take care of it, like getting the oil changed and stuff like that, but I was young and didn't know any better. As a surfer, I loved cruising the beach. In those days there were always some beautiful girls to look at. I admittedly was girl crazy. So was my best friend. We did a lot of cruising for girls, a lot of times while smoking fat joints.

There was a beautiful young blonde girl that hung out at the beach. She let me know me that she was interested in me and I was certainly interested in her. M was a high school girl and she certainly fit my profile and then some, but I resisted because I think she was just a little bit too young for me. But one day I stopped and talked to her. The next thing you know she's is in the Saab and I'm sitting shotgun. I don't know what came over me, but I'm a sucker for a gorgeous woman and she drove to my house. We had a problem parking and the Saab was wrecked, she was okay, but the chance of a relationship with her was slowly fading away. It's been five decades and there's still a mutual attraction, double unrequited love and her destiny unfulfilled, and like usual it's entirely my fault.

It was a while before I got a new car, so one day I was riding my bike by Star Park and noticed a little blue Corvette, I mean Corvair for sale (the car that made Ralph Nader famous with his book titled *Unsafe at Any Speed*.) Next thing I know, I was the owner of this baby. It even had baby blue moon hub caps. I bought it from the wife of Kirk K, my old buddy. It cost me $200 and I treated it like a throwaway car, but I had a ton of fun with it.

One of our favorite pastimes in those days besides looking for surf and cruising for girls was driving around Coronado smoking marijuana. One day, I had a great idea. We started driving on the sidewalk in front of the Coronado Shores, a waterfront high-rise ten tower condominium project. We probably did it a dozen times before anyone said anything to us, mostly because we caught them by surprise. Finally security stopped me and asked me, "What do you think you're doing?"

I told them, "I'm driving."

"You can't drive on the sidewalk!"

"It's a road."

I pointed to the sign which said no riding bicycles, no skateboards, no rollerblades and I told him, "It doesn't say cars."

He told me, "You can't do this anymore."

Being an obstinate teenager and a guy who loves to have a good time, I wasn't going let that stop me. In fact, it became even more fun now that we had someone to play with. So we continued to do it, but one day they must've been waiting for me because two security cops got in front of the Corvair and it looked like I was really going to have to pay a big price. Instead I leaned out the window and said, "Medical emergency!"

It was like parting the Red Sea. They just both got out the way and I drove right by, but this time I knew the gig was up and I was right. A couple days later there were two metal posts cemented into the ground on each end of the sidewalk. And every time I see them I say, "Those posts are for me."

After owning that baby for a year, the former owner approached me and bought it back for the two hundred.

THE BEACH COTTAGE

After CJ moved to Hanalei and after living with a friend for a while, I got this one-bedroom, one-bath cottage a block and a half from the beach, in two different directions. That was a huge break for me and I owe a million thanks too. That house was great for entertaining, and I did a lot of partying with beautiful women in that little cottage. I grew up a lot there and had many experiences whose memories will last a lifetime.

It was just off Star Park and a block from Coronado's downtown district, which was its own party scene. I was still waiting tables at Mulvaney's, and I was still working in the business. Since I was waiting tables, all the bartenders in Coronado thought I was at least twenty-one years old, leading me to a new form of entertainment. I still had the Washington connection, and it was valuable. Still, some other people in the business knew I had it and wanted to take it from me, but I ensured that didn't happen. There were lots of smugglers from Coronado, but good distribution is something most lacked. Now I had multiple connections to sell loads of marijuana to: three or four guys that I knew from Washington, Little Ricky and now I had a Salt Lake City connection, too.

Some of my other connections were down here in San Diego, some in South Bay, some in North County, and a lot were with people originally from Coronado. There must've been a hundred or so different organizations that originated from Coronado that were in the business. Some worked with others, and some worked alone. I was now one of the ones who was working alone, and it didn't bother me. I kind of liked it. I kept it low-key, unlike other people in the business, who were flashy on top of flashy.

BETSY B.

I think I was twelve the first time I saw her, and she stopped me in my tracks. She was so beautiful. I just stood there and stared. A few days later, I was back at Coronado High School to look for her, but I didn't find her. I saw the guy she was hanging with at the auto shop. That guy became her long-term boyfriend, and I would use him as one of my connections in the business. I would also see Betsy at my best friend's house because she was best friends with his sister.

A few times when Jimmy and I were out partying and ended up at the same function, we would get hugs from the older girls who were drinking and thought we were cute, even though we were four or five years younger. One time, when I was getting kilos from her boyfriend, he left me with her for almost two hours. Even though nothing happened, I think we both knew something would happen by the time I left with the load.

The next time I saw her, I was at the Del Coronado. I'd been drinking. She walked up to me and said, "You're not going to fall asleep on me tonight, are you?"

I said "No," but I was wrong.

I took her to the beach cottage and fell asleep on her, but it was on now and whenever she was down here and I could find her, we got together. This continued for years, even though I didn't see her often. She still had her long-term boyfriend, whom she always fought with.

After I retired from the business, I looked her up and found her in Bonita, where she lived with her long-term, still drug-dealing boyfriend. I went out there several times to hang out with her. She was so pretty and sweet. Long-term was still there, and they were still picking at each other all the time, but soon he was gone, and we started seeing each other again. We were mostly meeting for sex and companionship, but we started dating a bit too. Then, the business caught up with her one day, and she was gone.

BIG WAVE SURFER

After CJ settled in Hanalei Bay on Kauai, he invited me to do big wave surfing. I'd surfed some big waves before, or so I thought, like Swami's, Rincon, Seaside Reef, and many others, including the Tijuana Slough at twenty feet when I was merely thirteen. Now, I was going to Hawaii. I was nineteen years old, just a few weeks short of my twentieth birthday. I was stoked and jacked up, and I couldn't wait to get there. I'd always wanted to test myself on those big Hawaiian waves, and now I had a plane ticket.

I flew into Lihue on Kauai. The airport was like a time warp. The people waiting for passengers to arrive were sitting on bleachers, the kind you'd find at a high school football game. The baggage claim was outside with a tin roof over the top. It had probably been that way since they built the airport, likely around World War II. But it was pretty cool and unbelievably gorgeous flying into such a rural airport. The drive up to the north shore of Kauai was about a half-hour, and CJ had a fat Hawaiian Doobie that we smoked on the way. My head was on a swivel. There was so much to see and the kind of stuff I like to see: a spectacular tropical island, as green as green could be.

It was dusk, evening, and CJ suggested we go for pu-pu's (the Hawaiian term for appetizers) and a couple beers. We went to this place called the Anchorage down in Haena towards the end of the road. The last time I went there, it was called Charo's, after the Cuchi-Cuchi singer who bought it. It was a big, cool place; the beer was ice cold, and I could feel the Hawaiian good vibes. We'd been there about fifteen minutes and just got our pu-pu platter when Glenn K showed up. He came right over and greeted us; he was happy to see me and thanked me again for letting him clean a bale of stinky Hawaiian weed and supplying the labor at my house in Coronado.

He was a classic guy, always talking and happy. Being around him was fun. Then, a bunch of other Hawaiian guys had shown up and joined the ones Glenn came with. Soon, there were about a dozen of them, and they started pounding shots. We were halfway through our pu-pu platter when Glenn returned to the bar from his table with the dozen Hawaiians and said, "Hey, time for you guys to go."

I was confused. "We just got here and got our pu-pu's." Then CJ said, "No, it's time to go."

We left. I heard the next day the Hawaiians went after all the *haoles* (a term meaning "white devil" for white people in Hawaii), and it was all tables and chairs, cowboys and Indians. I'm sure some guys got their asses kicked because those were some big guys slamming back those shots.

Then, the next day, they were all out surfing like nothing had happened. It's the brotherhood of surfers because the waves were three or four times as tall as those guys. Thanks Glenn, for taking care of us! After that, CJ dropped me off at a shack in a cane field out in the middle of fucking nowhere. It was the shack where David Hamilton lived, the uncle of a future famous surfer, who was just a toddler. I was exhausted.

I'd smoked a lot of excellent Hawaiian weed and had a couple of beers, and I crashed right out. In the middle of the night, David Hamilton shot a rat off the inside of the roof with a .22. It was only one room. I may have been out cold, but not anymore. Certainly not what I'm used to. When CJ came to get me in the morning, I told him I needed better accommodations. It's just not working out with David and the crazy stories he told to me either, like getting shot in the back by an Orange County Sheriff when he was fourteen.

David belonged in Hawaii out in the sticks because he didn't belong anywhere else. He was there by default, as were a lot of people on Kauai. There were a lot of hippies living there for nothing at that time, and they had no idea how lucky they were to live in one of the most beautiful places in the world for cheap. Neither did I.

I went to CJ's house, said hi to Elizabeth (his wife), and picked up my baggies, surf trunks, and surfboard. My board was seven feet six inches and pretty pointy; hopefully, a good board in big Hawaiian surf. CJ told me it was fifteen feet at Hanalei Bay. I was stoked. So we got down to the beach, and you can see it's big, but you have to paddle through a bit of shore break and then out the channel to the reef, which was almost half a mile. I could see the surf was big, and as I paddled out, it kept looking bigger and bigger, but that's what I came for.

As I paddled through the channel, I could see the surf was larger and thicker than anything I'd ever been in before. These waves were unbelievably massive; you could see and feel it. It was scary, hairy, but gorgeous too. I had to go backside with my back to the wave instead of with my front to the wave, which I'd prefer. I was a goofy footer, and this was a right break, not a left. Yet, with the unbelievable power of these waves, you knew it would be death-defying.

These were ground swells traveling across the deep ocean, and suddenly, they hit this rock in the middle of the Pacific. Today, they're creating a monster wave with at least a twenty-five-foot face. Hawaiians say fifteen feet because they're measuring it from the back and trying to make you feel like it's nothing, thinking this isn't big surf. Well, I was going to be taking off on some death-defying waves and might've been in over my head, but I knew I wouldn't turn around and paddle back in. I was either going to make these waves surfing or take a pounding. That's what I came for, to challenge myself.

I got the lineup, and after about fifteen or maybe twenty minutes, CJ said to me, "This one's yours; go for it." I whipped my board around, paddled as hard as possible, and got up immediately. I was hauling ass along the top of the wave when I realized that I was going get pitched, and sure enough, I got pitched. It was like getting thrown off a three-story building, but at least I was landing in the water (that was the only silver lining I could think of).

I was unable to get down the wave because there was so much water being sucked back up, and now all that water was coming behind me to bury me. The ocean can be very unforgiving, and it would pound me mercilessly and I knew it. I got a good breath right before I hit the water and I found the reef right away by bouncing off it a few times.

The soup of the wave just kicked my ass, the kind of beating where you see your life flashing in front of you. It wasn't the first time this happened, but I'd never had a wipeout like that. Finally, I got my bearings and got back to the top. About four or five feet of foam there was there, and

I had to cut through it to get that vital breath of air I desperately needed. The first thing I saw was the lip of the next wave. It hit me right in the face and drove me straight back down to the reef again.

Still, this time, I landed on my feet and scrunched myself up to my knees, and I just held tight until the soup went by me, and I used my legs to spring back up. Soon, I was right back up to the surface where the foam was. I cut through it and got that breath, then swam for my life. I got under the next wave, popped up, and almost got sucked back over the falls, which is really the worst experience you could possibly have and probably would have been more trouncing than the last two waves.

Going over the falls happens when the wave breaks and you are already through it. Still, it sucks you back into the hole it just created, then churns you in the soup backward that's going over the falls. Getting sucked over the falls, that is the most awful thing you want to have happen to you when you're surfing, but luckily it didn't happen this time. I swam over the top of the next monstrous wave, and that's when I saw at least a dozen more monsters out there. All would have at least twenty-five-foot faces and looked like they were getting bigger and bigger.

So, I said to myself, I'm going to have to body surf one of these suckers. It might as well be this one. Then I turned around, swam right into it, and caught the biggest wave I've ever bodysurfed. I swear I have never been going faster in my life. I was flying and bouncing off my chest, and when I could hear that *crack* you hear when there's an enormous cloudburst. You hear that lightning *crack*, that's what I heard, that gigantic *crack*, and then it was like a huge earthquake, Ba-Boom.

Next, the wave hits the ocean, and I'm just swimming for my life, swimming with everything I have. When it gets me, I'm being shoved, but that's okay. I got my breath and I'm letting it push me forward. It's nothing like my first two churnings, but it would kill most mortals. The first two waves absolutely beat the crap out of me, and this went on for four or five more waves, and then miraculously, I was in the channel.

I'm just exhausted, like I've been run over a few times. I mean, my whole body is screaming. Then there's this big, huge Hawaiian guy, and he's got my board and says to me, "Hey, Brah, your board/"

I said, "Yeah, Brah, that's my board."

I didn't realize it, but they'd never seen any nonlocal body surf those twenty-five footers. Now I had instant credibility. I got the board back and paddled out behind him in slow but deep strokes. I was still trying to catch my breath, and I could feel all the muscles in my body working, but now it was starting to feel real good and I liked it. I could have said I was done for the day, but that's not what I came here for, and I wanted to get back out there, so I just put my head down and followed him. When I got back in the lineup, I could tell there was little scuttlebutt going on out there, I don't think they were expecting to see me again, ever. My host got some of that credibility, too, for not bringing any sissies.

That's when CJ paddled over and said, "Hey, Stu, you've got to paddle down the wave a little further before you stand up." The pounding I took had already told me, and I would have figured it out, but it was nice to hear it. So I set out for another fifteen or twenty minutes in the lineup, catching my breath and sanity. I now officially had more lives than a cat. The next thing you know it's my wave again. This time, I paddled down the wave a lot further, stood up, dropped in backside on a twenty-five-foot face (like jumping off the roof of a three-story building), and made my bottom turn.

I was hauling ass. The next thing I saw was the wave going over me. Unreal. I was in the tube for only a split second, and I don't think I've ever been going faster on any wave before. It was my reward for paddling back out and never giving up. I'd been in the tube before, but not on that big of a wave backside like that. I was flying.

I hung in there and enjoyed every second. You could feel the power, and it was awesome. Then, I kicked out probably a little too soon and had to paddle my buns off to get back in the channel. Another fifteen minutes later, I caught another one, and about fifteen minutes after that, I caught my third wave. Now the conditions were starting to change a little bit, and after riding the last wave for a while, I straightened off.

The soup pushed me into the beach. Tired and spent, it was time to get something to eat and time to sleep, and of course, CJ had a nice big Hawaiian doobie, so after I chowed down, I just rolled out that sleeping bag in the little shed and crashed hard.

That evening, we went to a surf spot called Pine Trees. It was head high, shoulder high, and pretty fast with many peaks. I got fifty or sixty waves. You could paddle right back out and get another wave even though there were fifty guys out there. The waves were everywhere, little peaks popping up all over the place. I certainly surfed my ass off again, and then the same routine: got something to eat, smoked some good bud, and crashed.

But what an excellent day of surfing! That's what I came for, and it was totally worth it. I hoped to do the same thing again the next day, but the waves weren't even one inch when I got down to the beach. It was absolutely flat as my girlfriend at the time, like Balboa, must've found it peaceful when he discovered and named the Pacific Ocean. So, now I knew I had surfed big waves, real big waves, changing my definition of big surf and now I could add Hawaiian big wave surfer to my resume.

The next day, there was no surf on the north shore, so CJ took me to the other side of the island, where he said he knew of a left break so I could ride the front side. As a goofy footer, I could go with my face facing the wave on a left break. I was out there for about twenty minutes. I'd probably caught about five or six waves when I told CJ, "The waters are a bit different on this side of the island."

That's when he said, "There's a slaughterhouse up the river, and you have to watch out for sharks here."

Oh lovely, we're like chum for those big tiger sharks. We didn't stay there long. Instead, we went to Brennecke's Beach, the best body surfing place in the world.

I bodysurfed for about two hours there. It's unreal, a perfect wave that lands you on the beach as the water peels away, almost like an out-of-body experience. I got to bodysurf there two more times on subsequent visits to Kauai. Still, in 1982, a huge hurricane (Iwa) went through Brennecke's, forever changing the bottom. The best bodysurfing spot in the world was no more.

I must say that my first trip to Hawaii was a success. Before the developers arrived, I'd never known how lucky I was to see this unbelievably pristine island. There was just this old road around the outside of the island; it twisted and turned with very little traffic. The only commercial buildings in Hanalei were the Ching Young store and the Tahiti Nui, and both had been there forever.

There was a restaurant bar called the Dolphin, and I went there for a few beers (the drinking age was nineteen in Hawaii). They had a huge picture window behind the bar, and they always ran water over the window, so it invariably looked like it was raining. People would think about leaving and then seeing what looked like rain so they could stay and have another drink. The drunker you got, the more it fooled you.

There was also the Tahiti Nui, but CJ told me not to go in there because the Hawaiians consider it their place and they will beat you up. Since I had already escaped a vicious beating at the Anchorage, I decided to heed his warning and stay out of the Tahiti Nui. In 1973, I decided that I would finally go inside. There was a small two-lane road that went around most of the island and not all of it was accessible, like the Na Pali coast. There was no Princeville, and we saw a red and white for sale sign nailed to a tree where they were selling half a Princeville for three hundred and twenty-five thousand dollars. The buffalo guy who bought that parcel had all the buffaloes across the Hanalei River.

I made many trips back to Hanalei. It's truly a magical place. I certainly entertained the thought of living there forever, but I was having a Peter Pan moment. There is definitely a lack of opportunity in the normal sense, and then there is the girl thing too. There are not enough girls to go around, and being a studley surfer isn't going to make a difference because there are many studley surfers in Hanalei. Not that you couldn't get one, but she would probably be cheating on someone. Me? I was just there to have fun, and I certainly did.

ISLAND MAGIC

My second trip to Hanalei was two weeks after my first. CJ lured me back with the promise of good surf and a good business deal. The surf wasn't as good as the first time but I certainly had tons of fun. I got to go to Brennecke's again and bodysurf that unreal world class spot. I mean, I still wake up dreaming about that place.

I also ran into a Coronado girl over there, and we decided to fly home together. She didn't know I had pounds of primo hash in my suitcase, but she knew something was up after we flew from Kauai to Honolulu. I told her I'd meet her at check-in because I needed to take a different route to get there. In those days, to get on a plane to the mainland, you had to go through the agriculture check, which was a hand search of your bag by US agents, and then you could proceed to the check-in for your flight.

I needed to avoid the agricultural guys, so as soon as I landed, I went upstairs. Just past the outer island terminal there was a small staircase you could walk up and into. It was the upstairs lounge in the international part of the airport. So that's what where I went. I sat up there for a little while. When I thought the time was right I reached into my pocket and pulled out the agriculture sticker I was provided with before I left Kauai and slipped it onto my bag. It was a sticky ribbon on one side and agriculture stuff on the other, now secured to my bag.

I sat there nonchalantly for another few minutes. I picked up my bag and walked down a different stairway that brought me right down to check in on your right, which is right in front of the agriculture guys on the left. I was still walking nonchalantly between them and right up to the check-in counter, gave them a killer smile and checked my bag to San Diego.

Got my boarding pass, went to my gate, and met my Coronado friend. I had a direct flight to San Diego and would be landing about one o'clock San Diego time. While I was standing there, people from United Airlines came up to me and asked me if I could give up my seat because an admiral needed to get back to San Diego.

I said, "No."

A few minutes later, they returned to me and said my seat was no longer on the plane. A food cart had replaced it, and I saw the Admiral and his wife walking by me on the other side of the fence. I recognized him because I'd been at his North Island house with my friend Jimmy Riley. He knew one of the daughters, and I knew the other, but she was smart enough not to have anything to do with us. They had a mansion with Filipino servants. You couldn't even smoke a cigarette without some guy sneaking up on you with an ashtray. Now he's taking my seat, and I've got my suitcase full of Primo hash and I'm flying under an alias so I couldn't make a big deal about it.

I asked my Coronado friend if she could pick up my suitcase for me because, obviously, I'm being screwed. She still had her seat, she agreed and it took another twelve hours for me to get a flight. However, it was supposed to be a direct to San Diego, landing around six o'clock in the morning, but as we flew into San Diego it was too foggy to land so we circled for a while and then they flew to LAX. Guess what? It was too foggy to land there. After circling for a while, they flew to San Francisco, and for some reason, on that one day San Francisco wasn't foggy so that's where they landed.

Now they're trying to hand me a reimbursement check in this fake name on my ticket so I can catch a flight back to San Diego. But they won't take that check because I don't have any ID. I mean, I do, but only one with my real name on it. So, I have to make up a bullshit story and tell him I put all my stuff in my suitcase that is waiting for me in San Diego. I told them I wanted to be hands-free and sleep on the plane, which was supposed to be in San Diego yesterday. I had a tough time advocating for myself, so finally, after a while, I got the supervisor involved and got on the plane. It was about time. I'd been in this for over twenty-four hours, and I was tired and wanted to get that suitcase and then some sleep.

Primo hash is probably the best in the world, especially if you get the surfboards and elephant ears patties (which I had). That's the old fashioned way. Those are century-old ways of making hash. The two different pieces are real thin ones that are long like surfboards and then these big fat one's that look like elephant ears. This hash originated in Kandahar, Afghanistan, and I don't know if it is available anymore (certainly not for Gringo smugglers).

You can watch hash being smuggled in the film *Island Magic* where they use a Winnebago to drive from Kandahar to Cape Town South Africa while filming a surf movie (their cover to transport the Primo). The big Winnebago was driven by the woman that CJ probably got the hash from. They had some excellent surfers with them, and the movie was a commercial success because there are a lot of unheard-of surf spots in gorgeous locations along the way.

Once they got to Cape Town, they sealed all the film inside the Winnebago and shipped it to Hawaii and customs didn't look inside because they didn't want to ruin the film. The film was made by a guy from Chula Vista named Orly and he was a friend of my friend Dave Charmers, who was famous for surfing with his dog Max (DC and Max). *Island Magic* is listed as a surf film, but it's really a smuggling film with some surfing. Oh, and it has a famous person in it too: the baby.

TWO GEEKS

While in Hawaii, I bought one of those crazy shirts T-shirts that said "elephant country" in smoke at the top of the shirt while showing a bunch of elephants smoking a fat joint. It was a fun shirt, and I could actually wear it at that age. I liked it a lot, and when the first one started to wear out, I got new ones on subsequent trips to Hawaii.

One day, I left the beach cottage and walked the block and a half to the beach to hang out with my friends wearing the older elephant country shirt. I was down there for a while, getting some future skin cancer, and then headed back to the beach cottage. About five minutes later, Big Al showed up and said,

"Two guys at the beach liked your shirt, and they wanted to trade for it."

I had a new one, so I asked, "What's the deal?"

"They have some hash, and I'll throw in this lamp I got from my grandmother."

I really liked the lamp. It was undoubtedly an antique with gold leaf swans. So the deal was made, and I put on the new shirt and headed back to the beach for more skin cancer. The two guys who got the shirt spotted me and engaged me in conversation. Apparently, they were street-level dope dealers from someplace in Orange County.

A couple of weeks later, I saw both of them on the rocks at Coronado Beach, and they saw me and signaled me over. I chatted with them again, and I ended up selling them a kilo of marijuana that I'd had left over. It was an old sample from our last smuggling effort, and I was happy to get rid of it. It was the first of about three or four times that I did that for those guys, and they were so happy to know a real smuggler. Plus, they were always super happy to see me, they made me feel like I had a fan club. Until then, they'd only known other dope dealers and no smugglers, and I could tell they held me in great esteem.

Well, it really wasn't the kind of business I do daily, selling one kilo at a time. Still, there was something about these guys. They were kind of goofy, and they appreciated knowing a real smuggler, so I decided I'd take care of them. I usually had a kilo or two that I'd prefer to have out of my house. One day, I was cruising the beach, and there they were on the rocks, like always, and because I had a sample in my house that needed to go, I pulled over. We did some greetings, and then I asked them if they wanted to buy the kilo, and they said they were no longer dope dealers.

"We're spies now."

I asked, "What do you mean you're spies, who are you spying on?"

"My father works at TRW (defense contractor), and we're stealing stuff from him and taking it to the Russian Embassy in Mexico City."

I said, "No, you're not."

They said, "Yeah, we are, we're spies."

At that point, I believed them, even though I hadn't known them for that long. They had a strange admiration for me and I'm sure they never lied to me.

They were two geeks who must've been selling the little bags of weed to their fellow geeks and now they're spies. I believed their story because they were so proud to tell me and wanted to share it with me. I think they drove all the way down here from Orange County to impress me, just to let me know that they were spies now and not just street-level dope dealers anymore. They elevated themselves and thought they were big-time spies working with the Russians. That was a big mistake on their part; they thought they knew me well, but they must have been confused by my happy-go-lucky personality.

TWO GEEKS

When I left them I went right over to my friend's house, my landlord's house by the little beach cottage. They allowed me to just walk in their house whenever I wanted to, within reason. I walked in, grabbed the phone on the long cord, walked into a private room, and called 411. I got the number for the FBI, called them, and told them the story. I don't think they really believed me, but I insisted this was true.

"You must have cameras in front of the Russian Embassy in Mexico City."

He said, "We don't have cameras there."

I said, "What about Lee Harvey Oswald and the Russians and their Mexico City Embassy? I would assume they had cameras there."

Then the FBI guy said, "What are you talking about? Lee Harvey Oswald in the Russian Embassy in Mexico City?"

"I don't think you know your history very well, but it doesn't matter. These guys are spies, and they are going down there and giving the Russians information stolen from one of their dads who works for TRW."

He asked me, "How do you know these guys?"

I said, "I'm a pot smuggler, and I sell them weed. But just because I'm a pot smuggler doesn't mean I'm not a patriot."

"Why should I believe you?"

"I grew up with kids whose dads were in the Hanoi Hilton, and I'm not going to turn a blind eye to this. All you have to do is set up cameras and wait for them to show up."

I'm unsure whether the guy really believed me when I hung up.

I would never turn in someone that I was doing a dope deal with no matter what; I'd take my punishment if I got caught. But these guys were no longer dope dealers. They were spies. Maybe they didn't notice the two Navy bases on either side of the island. They could see one from where they were sitting on the rocks, and you could obviously see the Navy planes landing at North Island Naval Air Station.

Coronado is my hometown. I grew up there with kids whose fathers spent years in the Hanoi Hilton, and there was no way I was going to let them get away with spying on our country. I don't know if I had anything to do with it, but I like to think so. They got busted, and some guy wrote a book about them called *The Falcon and the Snowman*. It made them out to be real big-time dealers, I guess. I've never read the book, but these guys were far from being any kind of big-time dealers. They were as small fry as you could possibly be. They were buying my leftover sample kilos, breaking them up, and putting them into little baggies that they sell for twenty bucks or something.

It's not big time or anything close; they're one level above street dealing. But in the justice system, almost every person who gets busted for drugs gets their status in the drug world elevated so the prosecutors can get them harsher sentences and climb the greasy pole of promotion based on how many people (our fellow humans) they put away for life or thirty years. That's how their promotion system works. I feel guilty for dropping a dime on them. I liked those guys, but those low-level dope dealers became spies and turned on their country; they crossed the line and got what they deserved.

I SHOULD HAVE KNOWN BETTER

I was a free agent dope dealer and domestic smuggler living in a little beach cottage, but now I was starting to get visits from other people in the business. One was Eddie Otero. He knew I had the Washington connection, and they could move copious amounts of weed. He also knew I wouldn't let them steal it from me as CJ did with Little Ricky, but they were persistent in trying to earn my trust to rip me off. Then Mike Acree started showing up. His brother and Eddie were the two founders of the Coronado Company.

The Acree brothers, Mike and Paul, were like two itchy brothers, and I soon found out why they liked heroin. Mike even left a little pile of it for me at the beach cottage. I wasn't interested in it, and it sat there for a week before Eddie showed up and thought I was doing it. I said, "Mike Acree left it there, and I'm sure he'll be back to get it. I thought he'd be back by now, but I'm sure he'll be back to get that in the next few days."

He tried to be a buddy with me, but that wasn't helping. The company could smuggle weed, but probably the best distribution deal they had was still Little Ricky, the connection they stole from CJ, and they wanted more.

Apparently, Eddie was back in the company after being kicked out. He replaced Paul Acree, who was kicked out for crashing his Pantera into a parked car and getting busted with a couple of ounces of coke and a derringer. Eddie successfully smuggled with Lights, so he was replaced with Eddie. Mike Acree showed up the next week and said, "My brother wants a meeting with you, me, and the big guy" (Paul's former lackey and new partner). All the principals in the Coronado Company either had Lackeys or followers (like Lance and Lou).

I met them at the beach cottage. They were looking to form a new company and offered me a partnership with a four-way split. I knew that the original Coronado Company was always split three ways, and that was the preferred split, so somebody in the four-way partnership that I stupidly was about to enter was going to be gone and looked like two brothers and one that was tight with them, so I possibly could be the odd man out. I knew to protect my distribution and would keep that to myself. I stupidly accepted their proposal and now I was partners with the Acree brothers and the Big Guy.

I was still doing my own thing, hooking up the Washington guys and sending packages to former Coronado people in Utah, Colorado, and New Orleans. That was profitable, but I didn't want to do that anymore. It was getting old.

Then my new partners told me they'd sent Mike Acree to Mazatlan to get kilos. He came back with a pile of coke that they were now trying to get rid of to get back to the original business of smuggling marijuana. I was not into smuggling or selling cocaine. I knew it had value, but that differed from what I wanted to do. I wanted to smuggle marijuana.

SET UP

I was in the beach cottage one day when a knock came on the door. It was an old Coronado guy named Jim Hughes. He asked me, "Do you know anybody with a couple of ounces of Coke for sale?" He knew someone who wanted to buy.

I told him, "No," but after thinking about it, I called the Acrees. Later, I found Jim and told him, "I might have some." The Acrees still had some that Mike returned from Mexico with when he was supposed to return with weed (I should have known that these guys were trouble).

I decided to help them get rid of the coke so we could get back to smuggling weed, and I didn't know how much capital they had, but I had some, that's for sure. So anyway, a couple of days later, he asked me again, and this time, he was with a tall black guy that made me suspicious. So again, I told him, "I don't think so" but he asked me to come over to his friend John's house the following week.

SET UP

When I showed up there was the same black guy but this time with a little kid, so I stupidly thought maybe I'd get a couple of ounces from the Acrees and help them get rid of this shit. I came back at a pre-determined time, and as soon as they opened the door, I could see the kid was gone and was replaced by an even bigger and thicker black guy. I knew I was in trouble, and the guy put a gun to my head right away before I even put one foot across the threshold.

He moved me over to the couch and kept the gun to my head the whole time. He told me he wanted the coke I had in my top pocket, but it was all flat, and I doubted he could see it, so I told him, "I don't have it with me."

He pressed the gun to my head, used it to move my head to the right, and told me that he was going to blow my brains out. I looked at John and Jim and shook my head. I knew these fuckers set me up, and I now I've got a gun to my head. So I said to the gunman, "Go ahead and shoot me. You'll never make it over the bridge."

He again said, "I'm going to blow your brains out," and even though they were like three blocks from the bridge, I've still got a gun to my head and I'm mouthing off like a motherfucker and I could tell they didn't know what to do with a son of a bitch like me. I was on the couch, and the thick black guy with the gun to my head was now standing in front of the couch with a coffee table behind him, and I knew that was a mistake.

SET UP

So I looked past him and, with a head fake, said, "Don't," and shook my head slightly, side to side. He turned his head to the right to look over his shoulder, which is the same side he had the gun to my head, so away from my head, the gun did go. I gave him a right forearm, and he went right over that coffee table. I jumped over the coffee table on his left and ran to the door; I got the two locks undone and pulled it, and there was a third lock.

That's when I felt a blow to the back of my head from the gun. I could feel blood squirting out of the back of my head, and I was seeing stars as I turned around and saw the bigger black guy standing now with the gun in his hand but down below his waist. He was waiting for me to pass out from the brutal blow to my now seriously bleeding head, but I immediately forearmed him again with my left because he was standing in front of the coffee table now. Some people never learn. He made a mistake thinking I was skinny, but I'm slim-thick, quick, fast and strong and I nailed him.

His big fat ass landed in that space between the coffee table and the couch, and he was stuck; Now I was running into the bathroom, and I dove through the window, just like in the movies, except it wasn't a movie window, it was an actual window with those little wood framed panes, little square boxes and I went right through them. I didn't have any choice, and now I'm bleeding from the back of my head and I was squirting blood from the front too. Then I'm out the window, and hauling ass down the alley, and let me tell you, I've always been fast, but that day I think I might've just been a little bit faster.

That's when I noticed I was in the alley where Paul Acree lived, and there was his house, so I put one hand on the top of his six-foot wooden fence, threw up my leg and with one move, I was over, much to the surprise of Paul. Paul's girlfriend was there, and she helped me stop some of the bleeding while he was lecturing me about jumping over his fence because he was on parole or probation or something. But then I told him the story, and he really couldn't believe it, so I said, "Look at my coat. Do you see the Coke?"

"No."

So I pulled the two ounces from my pocket and returned it. It was the first time and the last time I tried to sell any cocaine, but yeah, those two loser Coronado boys set me up.

I only wanted to deal and smuggle marijuana. I didn't want to deal cocaine, and there are lots of reasons why, like the one that happened there in that little alley. The original black guy showed up two weeks later at the beach cottage alone.

I told him, "What the fuck Bro, it's probably dangerous for you to be around here. It wasn't my shit," and then I said, "They know all about you." He looked at me, and I asked, "Really, what are you doing here?"

He looked at me like a deer in headlights, then I said, "You better get the fuck out of here, and you shouldn't be coming around here."

I never saw him again. Yes, smuggling cocaine for the Acrees was probably the worst thing they could do. They were big sniffers, and I guess they had a few pounds (I didn't know), but Mike seemed to be addicted to sniffing, whether it was cocaine or heroin.

SMUGGLING

The new company had a little meeting at the beach cottage again. It was decided that we would start buying weed in Mexico and smuggling it to the states and then I could distribute it, or they could distribute it. The partners were Paul Acree, Mike Acree, Paul Acree's former lackey known as Big Guy and me. They had two lackeys: Big Guy's little brother and someone known as the Blue Mule.

In retrospect, I should have stayed on my own, but I wanted a constant supply, and I needed some adventure. The partners, unbeknownst to me, were all using heroin. I had no interest in heroin or even cocaine, for that matter. Still, I was well aware that most of the women in that era who were out partying wanted some. I personally already knew people who had died from heroin use, not to mention one of my closest friends got on heroin during her first marriage and it ruined her life.

This new company didn't have many assets that were needed to be in the smuggling business. They/we were looking for a boat or a zodiac to start running the border in. Somehow, Mike Acree came up with a mark two zodiac, and I'm sure he swiped it from someone. We got it all set up with a powerful Mercury outboard. Now we were ready. All we needed were some kilos, which meant going to Mexicali, Mexico, or Tijuana. It was Mexicali, where we got a nice hotel room and called a local doctor in town known as Don Pepe. An hour later, he showed up at our hotel room with a nice-sized bindle of some very nice cocaine.

We gave him half of the money for kilos, and about two hours later the car we gave him showed back up all loaded and ready to go. We'd spent the last few hours snorting cocaine and watching Mexican soap operas in Spanish, not knowing whether we were going to be ripped off, shot and killed, turned in, or who knows what. Still, we got our kilos.

Next, we had to drive them to Rosarito Beach. We used three cars with the load car in the middle, one in front, and one behind, while we drove it to the Rosarito Beach Hotel. We passed such illustrious spots as La Rumorosa, a steep mountain road with a hairpin curve where buses and people have gone off the road and into a deep canyon some call the edge of the world. It was an old road built in 1917, but we made it to the Rosarito Beach Hotel without any problems.

We all had radios, and I was in the front car. Our job was to notify anyone of anything in front of us that might be a concern and if we had to ram someone so the load car could get through, that's the way it goes. Those in the rear car had the same job, possibly ramming as well, but nothing happened. We were all safe and left the car in the hotel parking lot.

A couple of days later, we showed up in the middle of the night and took over one of the cabins on the beach. Paul Acree, or Big Guy, had the keys from previous excursions to the Rosarito Beach Hotel. We got the kilos from the other car, put them in plastic bags, and sucked all the air out with a vacuum. We put the plastic bags into the sea bags, another plastic bag already inside, and sucked the air out again.

They were now pretty safe from getting wet, which was the idea because these sea bags were going in the Pacific Ocean. The bags were just a little over 300 pounds total, and four were there. And after getting wet, they would be around eighty pounds each. Next, we put sea bags in the Blue Mule's car trunk, took the old load car with us back across the border, and left the Blue Mule's car in the parking lot.

The next night, the Blue Mule was dropped off at the Rosarito Beach Hotel, and Mike Acree and I were in the old gold car with the Mark Two Zodiac and the Mercury outboard in the truck. We stopped at Punta Bandera and waited for the Blue Mule. He arrived about 15 minutes later, and we pulled the zodiac out and put it on the beach with the outboard and Blue Mule took the gold car back across the border and left the blue load car. Now it was time for Mike and I to inflate the zodiac, but Mike was already snorting heroin, and I was thinking, "holy shit fuckhead what are you doing?"

We got right after it, getting the Zodiac halfway pumped up with a foot pump when Mike started getting sick and puking. Now, I am inflating the zodiac alone when it's a two-man job. And Mike, he was still puking when he decided that he needed to do more heroin to get himself right. And I'm thinking, yeah, right, you gotta be kidding me, this is fucked up, and we are going to be late or get busted. Finally, Mike started helping me again; I guess he did need more heroin.

Good thing I didn't need any. We both had wetsuits on, and we finally got the Zodiac inflated to push it out a little bit into the water and set up the Mercury outboard engine; then went up and got the illicit cargo out of the blue car we then loaded the four sea bags, and we were off.

It was foggy, which was always good, but as soon as we came out of a big fog bank, it was dawn and the sun was not up yet…but it was coming up! We were fucked and had to change plans. I got on the radio and told Big Guy we were heading for underneath the bridge on the Silver Strand at the start of the state park, as it was the shortest distance from shore to the truck. Big Guy was driving the truck, and he was not too happy. We'd put him and everyone else in danger by being late.

Mike and I hit the shore in the zodiac, and it was on. I grabbed my two bags, one over my shoulder and one under my arm, and Mike grabbed his two bags, and I hauled ass to the truck. When I came to the first sand dune, two guys were in sleeping bags. I jumped right over the first guy; there was no way to stop my momentum. I was carrying a hundred and fifty-plus pounds in the two sea bags and had a lot of energy when I hit the truck and threw the sea bags in. Then I immediately turned around to see Mike with only one sea bag. He'd dropped one on the beach and had difficulty getting to the truck.

I instantly started running. I got the other sea bag, and when I came over the sand dune again, the guy in the sleeping bag was looking at me. I said,

"Looks like fun, huh."

I threw the sea bag in the truck where Mike was in the back as he tried to cover the sea bags with the tarp. He was also having difficulty doing that, so I jumped in to help him. Big Guy hit the gas, and it sent both of us flying out, and we got scraped up on the asphalt, and we deserved it. I picked up Mike and said, "Let's run."

Mike didn't want to run; he didn't care.

We got back to the zodiac and he nonchalantly cruised back to Imperial Beach where we had a van stashed waiting to load the zodiac. But there was no hustle, and Mike didn't give a shit. About fifteen minutes later, a Coronado police car arrived and asked what we were doing. We said we'd been diving for lobster. It was Officer Crooke, and he knew we were lying. Mike didn't hustle and could have cared less; I was pissed and felt he'd exposed me. We loaded the zodiac into the van we'd planted in Imperial Beach and drove back to Coronado. We learned that the load had been successfully dropped into a garage we rented off the 805 freeway in some apartment building's alley.

MIKE EATS IT

The new company had a meeting without Mike, and it was decided Mike Acree was too fucked up to remain a partner. After that, he went downhill fast and couldn't be trusted. He was ripping people off left and right and even lost his girlfriend, who was also all smacked out. She couldn't take the trouble that Mike had become (junkie couples usually stay together). A couple of months later, Mike died a horrible death in a hotel room in Tijuana.

A few years later, I ran into Officer McCool, who I'd known from my paper route. I asked him what happened to Mike Acree, thinking he knew because Acree's mother was the main dispatcher at the Coronado police station. Both Acrees told me numerous times that they'd gotten their mother to run license plates for them. I don't think I ever really believed that, but they insisted, and she loved them dearly even though she knew they were worthless criminals.

McCool told me that he was the one who took Mama Acree down to Tijuana to identify the body and bring it back to the states. I asked him how Mike died. McCool said with a needle in his arm, and it was filled with battery acid. Unfortunately, that's what happens to you when you're a total fuck up, and you think you can rip off anyone. He moved to Tijuana to get closer to the source (Heroin). If you think you can rip people off and get away with it in TJ and they won't care, you won't last very long.

Tijuana drug dealers are unforgiving when they figure out you're a low-life scumbag ripping off anybody to get his high. He paid for it with a death that must have been excruciating. His only value at that point was to be made an example of to others who were strung out in TJ. Yeah, it might be cheaper and more powerful in TJ, but it's also a place where life is super cheap.

I tried to talk to Mike after his heroin buddy Dave Gambrel overdosed, and Mike told me he wanted to get some of that stuff because it was so good it killed Dave. I knew then Mike was a lost cause; he'd lost his desire to live. He only wanted to get high. It was his personal search for the Holy Grail, but the holy grail was heroin. I knew it was only a matter of time before he died too.

SEA RAYS

Mike was out of the new company, and now we were at the preferred three-way split, but Mike took his Mark Two Zodiacs with him. That left us needing the boat, and soon we had one. Lance Weber and the Coronado Company let Paul Acree have their 24-foot Sea Ray, a powerboat that Lance had modified. He took one engine out and put two powerful engines in there where the one used to be. The boat didn't run right unless you had a load in the front, so until we got the weed, it was five fifty-pound bags of cement. The boat hauled ass though, and we took it everywhere down by Ensenada around Catalina and all over the coast.

I found out later when I was going to court that the boat had been bugged for location by the DEA the whole time we had it. I forget how many times we used it to smuggle marijuana, but we did a lot of reconnaissance. It's good to have a fast boat, an excellent plan, and the efficiencies that come with that. U.S. customs had three boats docked at Shelter Island: a Bertram and two Lipseys. If you had enough personnel, you could send a person to Shelter Island to see if they were in dock on smuggling night with a radio to let you know if they were out or not.

We got the 24-foot Sea Ray because the company got a new 30-foot Sea Ray paid for by Don Pepe. Whenever we would go to Mexicali to get kilos from Don Pepe, he would give Paul Acree a spoon of coke and then look at Paul and say,

"Where's Lou?" Lou Villar, head of the Coronado Company, promised to pay Don Pepe back for that 30-foot Sea Ray but never showed up with the money. Don Pepe made it known he wanted to kill Lou Villar. Don Pepe did large-scale deals on a handshake and expected you to honor it because that's how it works in Mexico. The penalty for stealing in the drug trade with Mexican kingpins is rather harsh, considering what happened to Mike Acree. I'm sure Don Pepe was well connected then. Later in my life, when I was the *Maitre d'* at the Chez, he came to the Governor of Baja Roberto de la Madrid's birthday party there. I recognized him right away, and I'm pretty sure he recognized me too, but neither of us said a thing, and that's how it's supposed to be.

One day, we had a quick meeting, and it was decided that we would get the next batch of kilos down in Mazatlan. The weed was fresher, better, and cost half as much, but it was a more dangerous journey. It was longer to begin with, plus you had to get by the drug stops all the way down on the mainland. You could see them on the other side of the road if you were going south. We had to deal with a charming character named Alex, a hard-drinking, very connected Mexican who grew up in Los Angeles but had to leave the country to avoid incarceration. Many Coronado people used Alex over the years, not just the Coronado Company.

We took a Coronado female smuggler with us who spoke Spanish. We outfitted an old International Harvester pickup with a camper and some brand-new boxes to put underneath for kilos. We had them specially made at a sheet metal fabrication place (Coronado Sheet Metal) used by many other smugglers. They were new and shiny, but we planned to rub grease all over them and drive them around on dirt roads to make everything look like it had been there for years. It wasn't my first trip to Mazatlan, but it was my first trip with the Big Guy. It would be the three of us: me, Big Guy, and our female translator. She tagged along to get a ride down to Mazatlan so she get to Cabo. We were also going to take the ferry, but we were going to La Paz with a truck full of weed underneath. All those checkpoints on the mainland road, well, there were none on Baja, so it paid to take the ferry even though it cost money.

MAZATLAN REVISITED

This wasn't my first trip to Mazatlan. The first time we were driving in a Volkswagen square back, the kind with the dual carburetors you could never get synchronized. The trip down was eventful. Our journey started by driving down Interstate 8 to Calexico, where we crossed the border and into Mexicali, Mexico. I was with two other guys, and the owner of the car drove the first leg through Mexicali and then it was time for me to drive. The other two guys fell asleep, so I drove all night long.

I was approaching Culiacan near daybreak when the vehicle owner woke up and decided it was his turn to drive. After sleeping all night, he decided that we were almost in Mazatlan. I told him we weren't and reached for the map to show him that we were not yet passed Culiacan. As I raised the map, the Volkswagen's square back slammed into a very slow-moving truck going the same direction as us (our driver fell asleep). I had neglected to put my seatbelt on when I changed to the shotgun seat, and I screamed as my head was going through the windshield.

The whole windshield came off, but some little string tied it to the car so now I was on top of the windscreen hanging on for dear life with my feet wrapped around and clinging to the dashboard. After what felt like an eternity, the car finally pulled over. I thought all my teeth were knocked out. Blood was coming down my nose from my forehead when I started spitting what I thought was going to be my teeth; lucky for me, I was spitting out those little chunks of glass about the same size as my teeth that you get when car glass breaks.

Then I noticed that the driver was bleeding from his forehead, so I pulled off my T-shirt, wiped the blood off my head, handed it to him, and told him to press down on his wound. The guy in the backseat was just fine, but we were in the middle of nowhere. The only building we could see was a big white one across the street, so we decided to walk there. We still didn't see any other buildings anywhere, but lo and behold, the building we did see was a hospital.

There was a long line of locals waiting to get in. I guess we were not thinking right and got in line behind them. A few minutes later, some people came running out of the hospital and were very concerned about our driver's wounds. Next thing you know, we were hustled inside. The driver got some of his head shaved, and stitches were put in his upper forehead. My forehead was wiped with a medicated wipe that took all the blood off, and I was fine.

But now we were still in the middle of nowhere, and the car was wrecked, and somehow we were in trouble for that accident (we were gringos). The big slow-moving truck never stopped, but we were responsible for the accident. That meant the Mexican judicial system was going to extract some money from the gringos. We got a room in a hotel called something like the El Ranchero in Los Mochis, Mexico.

The driver went to court the next day but was turned away because the judge partied too much the night before and was still drunk, and he closed the court for the day. That happened the next two days, too, so we left the driver and took a bus to Mazatlan. It was Carnival, and we wanted to have some fun after all our trials and tribulations with the car crash and the Mexican judicial system.

All the hotels in Mazatlan were full but lucky for us we ran into a Coronado guy named Chips, and he set us up with a guy who owned a restaurant called the Caballo Loco (Crazy Horse in English). It was perfect. We got to sleep on the floor after it closed, and that was good enough for us since we were drinking during the celebration and just needed to crash afterward. Carnival was over after a couple of days, and the driver showed up. Still, he had to return to Los Mochis because the judge hadn't sobered up yet.

The other guy and I took another bus to Tepic and then to San Blas. I liked Tepic, but we didn't stay there long, and by the time we got to San Blas my stomach was feeling queasy, probably from that fish taco I ate at the bus station in Mazatlan. I decided I should get some fresh orange juice while we were walking through the marketplace in San Blas. It was fresh squeezed and some of the best orange juice I'd ever had, but it didn't stay in my stomach long, and soon I was heaving it up on the side of the road while we were walking to our campsite. Montezuma's Revenge was upon me, and I was puking and pooping violently for days. I could hit a wall fifteen feet away from either side, and I was as delirious as a person could be. The other guy I was with was still not sick and was enjoying San Blas as I was lying on my sleeping bag and running to the bathroom every fifteen minutes or so.

One morning, I was lying in my sleeping bag when someone put a knife to my throat and told me, "Give me all of your money."

I told him, "Take whatever you want."

He rifled through my stuff while keeping the knife on me (there was no way I could defend myself, and he knew it), but he couldn't find any money, and it was now time for me to make a run to the bathroom. He kept the knife on me while I puked and crapped and cleaned up as best I could. Then, back to my sleeping bag with the knife still on me at my throat. He was now patting me down and found two traveler's checks, which he took. Our campsite was right across the street from the police station, and I've always thought my tormentor was a cop. About two hours later, a guy showed up—I swear it was the same guy—and gave me a pill to take. He told me that would make me feel better and where to get more in town.

I'm sometimes stupid, but I was delirious. I took the pill, and a few hours later, my misery was decreasing, so I reached into the bottom of my sleeping bag, got some of my money, and went into town and bought some more. The next day, I was back to my usual self and got acquainted with San Blas and I liked it, where I saw a boxing match and an outdoor movie all in the same evening. We never saw the driver of that Volkswagen again until we got back to Coronado. We rode the bus from San Blas to Tijuana.

BRAKE SHOES

The truck was outfitted, we had all our provisions, and it was time to go. Big Guy drove first, and then I got the wheel. After we stopped to eat, Big Guy and the female smuggler got in the back camper area and left me alone to drive.

I was passing all these big giant trucks to avoid problems with the oncoming traffic (lots of trucks coming both ways). It was slow and tedious, but I was trying to ensure my safety. At one point, I pulled out a little bit to see if the passing lane was clear. If so, then I'd pass one truck, get back in, start the process all over again. Once, I pulled out and didn't think I had enough room to pass the next truck, so I hit the brakes to get back into my lane and…nothing happened. The brake pedal went down the floor and absolutely zilch. I hit them again hard, and they locked.

That put the truck into a spin. With all these huge trucks coming at me, I thought for sure I was going to get killed.

BRAKE SHOES

Then we were launched backward off a thirty-foot embankment. The old truck landed on all four tires; none popped, and I brought that baby to a stop. I thought I'd done an incredible job of not getting killed, getting in a wreck, or hitting any of the trucks going the other way and landing on all four tires. Big Guy had a different opinion.

I hope they weren't screwing back there; that might have been really traumatic for both of them.

Big Guy says, "You're never driving again."

I replied, "I think the brakes locked or something."

That's when I looked up and noticed all the trucks on the road had stopped. All the truck drivers (there must have been a hundred or so) were out on the embankment's edge, looking down the thirty feet at us, probably wondering where the wreck was. Big Guy was still pissed, and I don't blame him, but it was the fault of the brakes, not me.

Big Guy checked the brakes. They wouldn't engage, so he decided I'd spoken the truth and announced that he had a certificate in break repair. We put the truck on a jack and took off one of the tires, then he went in there and rebuilt the brake on the side of the road.

He rebuilt all four brakes, one by one. Took about an hour and a half, and then we were back on the road headed for Culiacan. The Mexican highway had one lane each way and no shoulder and was much more dangerous than driving in the states. Luckily, the highway was not crowded.

BRAKE SHOES

We came out of Culiacan and headed down this steep mountain road. We were hauling ass when the Big Guy tried to brake the truck to slow it down...and again there was absolutely nothing, and we were going faster than that truck was built to go.

We could see in front of us a little bridge that looked narrower than the narrow road we were on. There was a guy with a donkey cart going our way in front of us and a semi-tractor trailer coming the other way as we approached the bridge, with no way to stop. The three of us were all in the front seat, and we were getting kind of worried, to say the least, as Big Guy could not brake the car in any fashion. He even tried to put it into reverse, but the clutch was spinning too fast and wouldn't engage. We were now on the bridge, flying. Big Guy was hitting the horn, and somehow or another, all three of us were abreast for a split second.

We were all screaming, and the semi tractor-trailer, the donkey cart, with our old international pickup in the middle, and all of us howled as we passed side by side. I don't know how it happened, but somehow, the three of us were all alongside each other when it didn't even look like two of us could be side-by-side. The bridge just expanded. I don't know how else to explain it. Well, I escaped death one more time in a matter of three hours since my last escape from death when we went off the thirty-foot bank backward. We finally got the truck to the side of the road in some dirt, which helped it stop, and Big Guy rebuilt the brakes again.

We inched our way into Mazatlan and got a hotel room in the older part of town, but still across the street from the beach. We dropped off all our stuff, showered, and went to find Alex with our female smuggler.

We found Alex in a bar in the older, all-local Mexican part of Mazatlan, away from the tourists. We all had to sit and drink with Alex and eat goat's liver that a guy barbecued right in front of us in the bar on a small hibachi. It wasn't the kind of stuff I would typically eat, but I knew not to say no in Mexico when offered something. It's considered rude, so *bon appétit*. It tasted okay when washing it down with a beer.

We told Alex about our brake problem, and he set us up with a mechanic who put new brake shoes on because that's what it needed, and it cost us eight bucks. Best eight dollars we spent on that trip. After that, we dropped the female smuggler off at the ferry and went to meet Alex again. We gave him half our money and he told us to stay at least two miles behind him as we went off into El Boondocks, somewhere in the sticks on the rural backside of Mazatlan.

It's always the same: are we going to get robbed or killed, and are we going to get our load? Well, Big Guy didn't hear him too well, or he didn't care because he wasn't even close to staying at least two miles back from Alex. I questioned why he wasn't following directions, and he said, "That guy's got half our money."

True. I already knew that, but I like to follow directions. When I'm in a foreign country picking up contraband to smuggle back to my country, it just seems prudent.

I once knew a beautiful woman who was arrested in Mazatlan. She was groped in a bar and shoved the guy. She told me he was an obese slob, a fat, nasty, old, ugly Mexican man, who fell back, hit his head and died. Still, when there's trouble in Mexico, and it's between a Gringo and a Mexican, the Mexican always wins. Later, the Mexican police tortured her so much and so often, she couldn't have any children. That's the famous torture you get with a cattle prod in Mexico, and years later, she jumped off the Coronado Bridge. Rest in peace, sweet Annie West, you were a beautiful woman.

YELLOW RIVER

It wasn't long before we got pulled over by the cops. The Big Guy said,

"I'll handle this."

I knew it was the cops right away because the guy who seemed to be in charge had a pearl-handled pistol on his belt. The crooks in Mexico that have guns don't keep them on their belt, and they don't have pearl handle pistols because when they shoot someone, that gun needs to disappear. If you're a cop, you just put a notch on it.

Big Guy immediately said, "We're friends with Alex."

That started a little panicking in me because I knew he was talking to a cop, but I'm not sure he did. So I jumped out of the car and said, "Alex helped us with our brake shoes, *zapatas de freno*, (brake shoes in Spanish).

The guy looked at me and said, "I went to San Diego State."

Interesting way to let me know that he knew both languages and that we were fucked as his underlings decided they were going to search the truck. We had a readily observable false bed in the back of the truck where we put camping gear and tools, and they found that right away.

Big Guy told them: "There's nothing in there but camping gear and tools."

When they discover that false bed that you can easily find, you can tell they get excited because they think they've got us, but I think it's even more deflating when they find out it's just tools and camping gear like we told them. Usually, the search is over after that.

But they found the nice shiny new metal boxes underneath the truck, which was a total bust. Now the guy that's got a pearl-handled pistol has it in his hand and puts it to my head, looks at us and says, "Do you have any guns."

"No."

He knew we were smugglers now, but I wasn't all that worried for some reason, maybe because of how things were being handled, and he hadn't arrested us. It was about then that Alex appeared, and the guy that went to San Diego State, who I believe was the head honcho, went off to the side with Alex, and they talked for about ten minutes. Then Alex returned to us and said,

"Everything's okay, but you should've stayed back two miles like I told you."

We asked him how he fixed things. He told us the San Diego State guy with the pearl-handled pistol that his father works for him (Alex). I'm pretty sure some money changed hands, but not that much. But now we're back on the road and this time we stayed back like we were told to. Later we see Alex by the side of the road. He directs us into a batch of trees on a dirt road, and we now have our kilos. He started singing "Yellow River" because he named his weed that and he was drunk, but he wanted us to know how good it was. It was much better and fresher than the weed we were getting from Don Pepe in Mexicali.

We packed them in plastic and put them in the sheet-metal boxes underneath the truck bed. Then we smeared grease all over them and drove the truck around on the dirt road for about 10 minutes. We checked underneath, and everything looked like it had been there for years. We returned to the hotel, dropped off the truck in the parking lot, and walked down to the Playa de Mazatlan. It was a huge fancy hotel where we sat down for a late lunch, and Big Guy started drinking. I had one beer and a wonderful lunch with a gorgeous ocean view. It was just lovely, and when the bill came, Big Guy wrote on it a twenty percent tip to room 507.

That made me a little uncomfortable with our truck loaded with three hundred pounds of weed underneath at our hotel. Still, Big Guy said no problem; he'd done it before. Hence, we just rolled out of there, walked down the boardwalk passing Senior Frog's before it was famous to our hotel and crashed.

ROSARITO BEACH HOTEL OR BUST

The following day we headed to the ferry. As we came around the corner, we were already in a coned car line, and there was an inspection going on with Mexican customs. Holy. Fucking. Shit. All kinds of stuff started going through my head: Did the San Diego State guy screw us or Alex? You never know in the drug world. We'd checked with other Coronado people who'd made the trip as little as two weeks ago. This was the first time we knew or heard of an inspection at the ferry. We had one thing going in our favor: the Mexican guys usually didn't want to get down on the ground and crawl underneath the truck. Still, we did it right as far as we knew, and we'll have to roll with it.

There was no backing up, and Big Guy already had a cocktail (I wanted one too now) while driving, which made me nervous. Then, right next to me, there's a *Federales* getting down to get under the truck, and I wasn't going to let that happen, so I opened the door and hit him in the head with it. That caused a huge ruckus, and I almost got arrested right there, but I offered them all cocktails.

They believed us to be fools, and they didn't go underneath the truck because they found the false bed in the back and were so excited. But just like the San Diego State guy, we told him there was nothing in there but tools and camping gear, and when they opened it, they became flaccid again. They found the tools and camping gear. You could taste their disappointment. It was like a trick. It was easy to find and always worked in our favor. Finally, they'd had enough of us and let us go, and soon, we were on the ferry headed for La Paz. It was just another day smuggling weed.

It took all night for the ferry to get to La Paz. Big Guy drank a little while I didn't. I talked to a couple of people on the ferry, and they told me about some ferries disappearing in the Gulf of California. That left me slightly nervous, but we arrived safe and sound. Now we had to drive to the Rosarito Beach Hotel. It would take us the entire day and part of the night. We got a tank full of gas and noticed we were running a little short on money as Alex cost us a little extra (bribe money). We had enough money for both of us to get a good meal somewhere on the way home and another tank of gas.

We talked about going to the famous taco stand were all the Coronado smugglers stopped with their loads on the way back to Rosarito or wherever they went. We decided against going to the taco place (it might be hot by now). We ended up at a fancy French restaurant in Santa Rosalia, or so we thought. We were starving and about to get the worst meal we had ever been served. The bread and the Coca-Cola were pretty good, but I was still starving.

My fish tasted like it had sand in it. I've never tasted anything as horrible, but a close second was the meal I had with Paul Acree on the Queen Mary. Salmon with lots and lots of bones and a curry sauce that was not edible. After our meal it was time to get back on the road again. It was dark and we were tired before we got to Rosarito Beach Hotel. We went into the hotel lobby and called to get the Blue Mule to pick us up. We left the truck in the parking lot, where we could easily retrieve it in a day or two.

FLATFOOTS

The next day, we were back at the Rosarita Beach Hotel in the middle of the night. We got the kilos from underneath the truck and brought them to the usual beach cottage. We wrapped the kilos in plastic, sucked out the air with a vacuum, and then packed them in more plastic in the sea bags. Then we put the sea bags in the trunk of our load car, left it in the parking lot, and took the truck back across the border.

The next night Blue Mule dropped Big Guy and me off at the Rosarita Beach Hotel. We hopped in a load car and drove down to Punta Bandera. We got out of the car and went down to see if we could see the 24-foot Sea Ray. Not yet, but we decided to get into our wetsuits and get the four sea bags down to the beach below the cliff where they couldn't be seen. In a few minutes, we spotted the Sea Ray with Paul Acree driving. Big Guy and I tied the sea bags to our ankles with ropes and entered the water, dragging the bags into the water after us.

The sea bags floated really well, so we swam through the shore break and out to the Sea Ray, climbed on board, and hauled in the square fish. Square fish were the easiest fish in the world. To catch them, you go off the coast of Mexico, blink your flashlight a couple of times, and they're jumping on board the next thing you know. We untied the rope from our ankles and the sea bags and got them ready to jump.

The 24-foot Sea Ray could haul balls, and it was only about five minutes before we were off the coast of Largo's (right where the new Navy Seal base entrance is) on the Coronado Silver Strand, our designated jump spot. There was only one problem: two Japanese guys were fishing right there, so we jumped another quarter mile north.

This would mess up our pickup by a van driven by Big Guy's little brother. We worked our way through the dunes, keeping low so as not to show a profile. And here comes the van, which drives right by us because he's looking to pick us up at Largo's.

Five minutes later, he drove by again, and this time, his big brother hit the van with a rock, but that didn't stop him and it happened again about five minutes later when we hit him with the second rock. Big Guy decides to go down to Largo's and tell little brother we're a quarter mile north. I was lying beside the four bags on my stomach when I saw the police lights. Then I could see the cop talking to the Big Guy because of his big ass profile. I didn't freak out. I just found the nearest big sand dune and started digging out the bottom with both hands and feet.

Soon, I had a nice trench, big enough for all four sea bags. I put them in there, and it kicked all the sand back over them; it looked perfect. I returned to lying on my belly and saw the cop light still going around at Largo's. I thought about burying myself, too, but then the lights went out a few minutes later, and then I could see Big Guy walking up the Strand. I still wasn't moving, but I watched him go to the little hut at the Coronado Cays entrance. About ten minutes later, the taxi arrives, and Big Guy gets in.

I looked both ways, jumped over the fence and hauled ass, and jumped in the opposite side door in the back of the cab. This taxi driver had two guys in wetsuits coming from the Coronado Cays, I always wondered what he was thinking.

I asked Big Guy, "What was the deal with the cops?"

"I told them, my friends, who I was diving with off a boat, thought it would be funny just to leave me in the water all by myself. I don't think it's all that funny."

The cop said, "You really shouldn't be down here in a wetsuit; because this is a known smuggling spot."

We both thought that was pretty funny.

FLATFOOTS

We returned to one of the houses in Coronado, where we all showered up and then met up with Blue Mule, little brother, Big Guy, and Paul Acree at Marco's Italian Restaurant. Then we drove three cars down the *strand* and successfully picked up the four sea bags. Big Guy and I jumped out of the first car with Paul driving, found the sand dune, dug up the sea bags, got them by the road, threw them in the middle car (the van), then jumped in the third car and ensured no one was behind us. The front car made sure no one was in front of us. We were done for the night as the van with the sea bags was going to the safe garage off the 805 in mid-San Diego.

CARDIFF OR BUST

At a meeting of our little company, it was decided I should move from the beach cottage in Coronado to a newly rented stash house in Cardiff. So, I moved out of the coolest little house about a block from the beach in Coronado and rented for one hundred dollars a month and loved living there. We were now scouting spots in North County to land loads from the 24-foot Sea Ray. Most of North County had cliffs, which were good for hiding smugglers and their loads.

The Cardiff house was where Judy Jordan came and spent the night with me, and when my partners found out, they were pissed. I don't know why, but they didn't like Judy and thought she would harm us all. I tried to convince them otherwise, but they would never be convinced for some reason. It was nice to hang out with my first girl again because I loved her dearly. Interestingly, Paul had a tight relationship with Lance Weber, and Lance loved Judy, too.

To keep tabs on the police, we purchased two Bearcat scanners with two car battery inverters. We put them in vehicles and then listened and deployed them on pot running day. Each bearcat had sixteen channels; you could program them to whatever crystal frequency you wanted. After we paid cash for them at the Mission Valley Radio Shack, the clerk asked us, "Are you guys dope dealers or smugglers?

I gave him a shocked look and said, "Neither." Acree said, "Both."

Then the guy reached under the counter and handed us three pages with all the crystal frequency of all the police departments and all the federal agencies in town, such as Customs, Border Patrol, Coast Guard, DEA, FBI, and all the local police departments. That helped even more. We were already spying on the Customs boats they kept by the marine fuel dock on Shelter Island and the airplanes they kept on North Island, where we could eat at Air Island Café and check them out. All my partners had dads who'd done time in the Navy, and we had no problem getting on the base.

SANTA CRUZ

We had plenty of loads in that Cardiff house and in a couple of the closets the floors were covered with marijuana seeds. We leased the property for one year from a couple of gay guys who kept on telling me how much more they like to rent to men rather than women; they said women are so dirty and filthy. After they told me that four or five times I thought maybe I should ask them for a list of those women with their phone numbers because they were starting to sound like they might be my kind of girls.

About halfway through our lease, the 24-foot Sea Ray disappeared. We had been stashing it all over San Diego County, in and out of the water, but we didn't know that the whole time we had it, it was bugged for location by the DEA. I forget how many times we landed loads with that boat. Still, it seems ridiculous we never got caught considering it was electronically tracked for location 24/7. Still, we did a lot of recon in that boat, too, so we might've confused them by not landing more times than we did land. Now, we were amphibious assault-based smugglers. We had no boat.

About a month and a half later, we heard that the DEA had also seized the Coronado Company's 30-foot Sea Ray, and both boats disappeared. Things were changing again. We were looking for a boat to use when we got word that the company had thirty tons of weed all in kilos at sea in a tuna boat. Big Guy, little brother, and I were offered jobs with the landing crew. I declined, but the other two went for it. They first tried to land in Santa Cruz, but the surf was about ten feet. They almost drowned little brother, so they went back to the spot they were more familiar with and with smaller surf around Point Mugu.

A few days later, I flew into Santa Cruz with Baby, who I hired for $150 to help me drive a big yellow Ryder truck full of kilos to Washington State. We flew into San Jose and waited for Paul Acree to come down route 17 and get us. It was a funny scene at the airport while I waited for Paul to show up in his rented Camaro. It was like an all-class reunion from Coronado High School. I kept seeing all these Coronado guys and they were all saying the same thing: "Don't tell anybody you saw me here."

Everybody was coming to get their kilos and take them somewhere; too bad the company already had little Ricky, or I'd be sending him some kilos too. Their quest to get the

Washington guys from me was put on hold because they were so busy trying to get rid of their thirty-plus tons of weed. They had never smuggled anything even close to that much weed, and they needed a lot of help getting rid of it.

One of my friends said he saw two Coronado guys in the airport wearing wigs, which was so obvious too. We had a connection in Santa Cruz; he sold over five tons of that weed for us and them, and we all made money on those loads. Soon, I was in another yellow Ryder truck heading back to see the Washington guys. We sold over a ton to them.

It was a lot of weed for them to handle, but everybody was flush with cash, and we were selling tons of marijuana. The company did two more loads from Mexico in those tuna boats and we got to sell a lot of weed for them. We had different styles. Acree drove around Santa Cruz in a Camaro. I went around in my blue or green polyester leisure suit in a Crown Victoria. Paul looked like a fucked up drug addict and dope dealer, and I looked like a cop (well, a stoned cop). At that time, it seemed like everyone in Santa Cruz was a dope dealer of some kind.

THE SPLIT

And then it was over. Big Guy and little brother decided to split off to hang with the guy in Santa Cruz who helped us sell over five tons on the first load. Paul Acree and I decided to look for a new boat. The big question was whether we would get a fast or slow boat. Customs was on to fast boats, and they had some of their own now. I was watching the local news when I was back in San Diego. The head of customs was visiting San Diego and they took him out on a boat in the middle of the night, down to the border, and a bunch of zodiacs whizzed right by them. That's when he went on the local news and said he was going to stop all those "God Damn Tijuana Boat Races." And then both the Sea Rays got seized by customs; we didn't even know where they disappeared to, so maybe fast boats and trying to outrace the cops might be ending—but trying to find a place to hide the boat was getting more difficult. In a slow boat, you could go outside and around the present search zone for fast boats, but if they're on to you, you'll never be able to outrun them. Slow boats are easier to hide because they usually have a work or pleasure component or function.

Deception has always been part of the smuggling way of life, but with Paul, it was apparent he wasn't a yachtsman or worker. Paul was leaning towards a slow boat (because that's the direction Lance Weber was pushing him), but we were looking at them all.

About that time, the Coronado Company, or maybe just Lance, hired Paul to scout the west coast for landing spots. Paul told me they were going more international and not looking to smuggle from Mexico anymore. I went along with Acree, and we traveled down the coast. We looked at a few places in Washington, mainly around Astoria. We scouted all of Oregon, found a few good spots, and explored California down to Santa Barbara.

Traveling with Paul Acree was not very entertaining. He had a big bag of coke and another of heroin, and he was screwed up all the time. Not only that, but he was the biggest asshole I've ever traveled with. Whenever we went out to eat, he had a habit of pissing off half the people in the restaurant. That got old quickly. Even though we were doing business together, I hadn't been hanging out with him. He hung out with Big Guy and their smack buddies. I wasn't doing any heroin, but I did go to a big dope dealer party in Santa Cruz with my partners at the guy's house that sold the five tons for us.

I'd never seen so much cocaine in my life! They had piles of it everywhere. my partners were in heaven, me... I was wondering where all the beautiful women were. You can't have a good cocaine party without them. Still, for some reason, all they had was dope, and that made it pointless for me. I liked to party with beautiful women, not just get all messed up.

They were doing huge lines. I had a few myself, and I must admit it was pretty good stuff. Nobody was stepping on this shit as it didn't come from a street or bar dealer. But the party was all dope dealers and not that fun for me, (no beautiful women), and I think that's where I got that stigma against coke. Years later, I was the best man for Baby at his first wedding, and there were lots of Chart House guys there and each one had a big bindle of the evil white power. I think they had even more coke than all those drug dealers in Santa Cruz. I didn't have any coke, and I didn't miss it either.

I think it ruined the atmosphere because everyone was trying to find a place to do coke instead of engaging with their family members and all the non-cocaine people who came to celebrate the couple. Still, they weren't available because they were off doing coke. I thought it was really weird and I left. Cocaine ruined the lives of so many people

I know. It was the biggest fad of the 1980s. Everyone was doing it, even Republicans and people you would assume would never do cocaine were doing it, some all the time. It broke up marriages, ruined businesses and friendships, made people homeless, and earned the name *Evil White Powder*.

EATING SPIT

I ate out with Paul all the time, and it was always the same: He would find a way to piss off the staff and the tables all around us. At first I was amused, but it got old rather quickly, but even then, I was amazed that he never changed his tune. I'm sure he ate a lot of spit, and I probably got some, too, for hanging out and protecting him. The Fucker. Once in Marina del Rey, Acree and I were out for dinner at a restaurant when Paul pulled out a wad of money and spread it across the table. It was all tens and twenties and probably around eight hundred bucks, covering most of the table. Then he told our waitress to send all the pretty girls to our table and asked her which bill she wanted. She took a twenty, and then all the pretty girls that worked there started to come by and chat us up and flirt with me, but not gnarly Paul, but to their credit they did try to be nice to him.

It was a huge, beautiful restaurant with many pretty girls who all came by to get their twenty, except those who only qualified for a ten. I must admit I had a perfectly enjoyable time and was able to snag one of the pretty girls, but I came with Paul, and we all left in the rented Camaro, with her in the back seat because she didn't want to sit with Paul.

I think Paul immediately offered her drugs like cocaine, probably not heroin, and I fired up a joint of Thai weed, which she took a few hits from. Soon, Paul was driving crazy down Admiralty Way, and it wasn't long before my prize realized she'd made a mistake, and we had to take her back. I wondered what took her so long. Paul was getting really bad and I didn't blame her, but I did blame him and knew I had to get away from him.

FISH HARBOR

Paul Acree and I started going to boat shows. The first one we went to was in Newport Beach, and we went to a couple in Long Beach. We weren't a mystery to those in the boating world. They knew just by looking at us that we were smugglers, but most were willing to work with us because they wanted our money. Still, a couple of times, the hoity-toity yacht brokers wouldn't let us on their boat, and I'm blaming that on Paul because he always looked so fucked up. I remember we walked up to one yacht, and the sales agent looked at Paul and me and said "uh-uh" while holding his hand out in the stop sign position. Acree and I liked the Fisher 38 trawler, but we would've been out of place showing up with that boat.

We found an old jig fishing boat, the Patrick, the owners had converted to fish for giant squid. They caught giant squid by going out at night and shining bright lights on the ocean, and the squid would come up, and they'd snag them. I was skeptical. The boat was old, and there was no way it would out run anyone, but Acree liked it and he had Lance look at it. Soon, it was ours, but the new owner was Paul's mom. We put it in her name. We had to find a place to dock or moor our new boat. It was a diesel and had this one huge engine, a GMC 671 HN9, the same ones they used to power military bases in Greenland. We bought it from some nice old guys who used to be probation officers. No doubt, they knew we wouldn't be fishing for squid.

We found a place to hide the boat at Fish Harbor, just a little south of San Pedro. It was called Fish Harbor because it smelled like fish and was full of tuna boats and canneries. I told Acree that San Pedro could be like Coronado if they cleaned it up a little, but we were in Fish Harbor. The only thing west of us was Terminal Island Federal Prison, Lance's old home. Hanging out with Paul Acree was starting to worry me, with all his hardcore drug use that never stopped, and I had to look at Terminal Island every day hoping it wouldn't be my new home. Fish Harbor was where all the tuna boats unloaded their catch, and it reeked of fish, which is why we were able to find the dock space to moor our boat. It was the only one with availability in the Los Angeles area.

We were taking the Patrick out and test-driving it. We ran it around Catalina several times but never went ashore.

We were getting ready for Mexico. Most of the time when we were in town, we crashed out at a Holiday Inn in Long Beach, but every once in a while I wanted to get away from Acree so I would sleep on the boat. That happened more and more as time went on.

There was a bar about half a mile away that was supposed to be a rough and tough Longshoremen's Bar. Acree used to say when we drove by it, "If you want to get your ass kicked, go there at night and drink." So one night when I was staying on the boat, I walked to the Longshoremen's Bar and I didn't get my ass kicked. I had a great time and walked back to the boat kind of drunk. I got up the following day, and there was a boat tied to ours, and it had stickers all over it saying this was the property of U.S. Customs and trespassing was not allowed.

What do you know? I had a 30-foot Sea Ray tied up to the Patrick. I'd heard of this 30-foot Sea Ray before, but I'd never been on board; however, that was about to change. Even though it had all these stickers all over it saying not to go on board, that just made it more inviting, so I decided I was going to take a look inside. They had a security guard at Al Larson's Marina; he was there every day and another every night.

So I sat there and waited for him to come by, and he came by at twenty to the hour, and the next time he came by, it was also twenty till. At ten to the hour, I entered the

30-foot Sea Ray, and the first thing I saw was the leather skullcap that I knew belonged to Lance Weber, so I picked it up and shoved it in my back pocket. I got out of the Sea Ray, jumped in my car, and drove into Long Beach. I found Paul at the Holiday Inn, and I told him, "I found the company's 30-foot Sea Ray."

He looked at me like I was insane, but I wasn't the one that was all fucked up on drugs all the time.

"No, seriously, I found it. Well…it found me."

Paul asked, "What do you mean?"

"I woke up this morning, and I found the 30-foot Sea Ray tied to the Patrick with a bunch of custom stickers all over it saying Property of US Customs do not enter. That was like an invitation, and I went in there and checked it out." I reached into my back pocket and pulled out Lance's leather skullcap.

Acree recognized it. "Really?"

"Yup. It looks like it has a nice radar on it, and that rader would look even better on the Patrick."

A couple of days later Acree got word back from Lance that he had the original receipt for the radar, with the serial number, under the name of Edwin Hull. That was Lance's marine and boat alias. So, Acree and I decided we would steal it. Was it really stealing? We would have the original receipt because the guy who bought the radar was giving it to us. It just happened to be in the temporary possession of US Customs.

So, I got up at 1 a.m. and started to watch out for the night rent-a-cop. He came by every hour at ten after the hour. So, I was back in the 30-foot Sea Ray at three thirty in the morning. The radar counsel in the cabin would be easy to remove; it had a thick cable but I cut it. Then I got up on the tuna tower to try and remove the antenna part of the radar. That was to be more complex because when I turned the bolts on the tuna tower, it wouldn't unloosen the nuts underneath; they just spun.

There was no way on earth I could turn the bolts and secure the nuts so they wouldn't spin without getting more equipment. So I put the radar console back where it was, even though I'd already cut the cable. I cleaned up my little mess, and the next day, I went to the hardware store and bought two vice grips and some PVC piping. I got up at 1 a.m. to watch the night watchman the next night.

He was consistent. He came around at ten after the hour, so I went back on the 30-foot Sea Ray. I pushed the two vice grips into the end of the PCV piping. I clamped the grips on two of the four bolts underneath the tuna tower, so when I turned the bolts from the top, they would still spin the nuts until the PVC pipes hit the tuna tower poles, and then I could undo the bolts. That made it easy. I got two of them off, and then I got the other two using the poles and vice grips again, and we were ready to go.

Acree also slept on the boat that night so he could help me. I put the radar antenna on a rope and lowered it down to the deck of the thirty-footer and then I went back and got the consul. Then Acree came up, and I handed them to him one at a time. Then I cleaned up everything on the Sea Ray, and we put them on the Patrick. We pulled up anchor, untied the ropes, and headed for San Diego.

A couple of days after hanging out in Coronado, I went over to the Patrick. It was like a radar installation party. Lance and Henry (The Lance from the Point Loma Company) and my old buddy Al Sweeney were there. Lance was surprised when Al greeted me with, "Stu Daddy, how's it going?"

Lance asked, "How long have you guys been friends?"

We both looked at him and laughed, and I said, "Nursery school."

"That makes sense."

It was nice to see Al working inside that cable I cut. There were a hundred and thirty-five little wires, all different colors, which my old buddy Al was splicing back together with a new cable, and soon the Patrick had excellent radar. After installing the radar, Paul Acree came to me and offered me a buyout from Lance for fifteen thousand. I should've taken it because I was getting sick of

Acree. He was such an asshole, and he was all fucked up all time, but it wasn't enough money and no one made a counteroffer. Now that Lance, Al, and Henry had helped us with the boat, it seemed to be running much better, and we started going to Mexico.

MORE SPIT

Hanging out with Paul Acree was getting uglier, just like him. He was becoming increasingly belligerent and I was getting tired of being stuck in the middle, of being the one who had to defend him.

He always liked diving Camaros from Avis or Hertz. One time when we were in LA, we were getting on the freeway on one of those cloverleaf on-ramps. We seemed to be going around for too long when the front driver-side right wheel came off the vehicle making metal to pavement sparks. We were blocking the on-ramp, and when the CHP came by, we told him they needed to get in touch with Avis and have them bring us a new Camaro, and that's just what happened. Then Acree was all super aggressively antagonistic. He took that new Camaro they dropped off and purposely started wrecking it, by doing things like slamming it into reverse when he was driving too fast to start with. I'm sitting shotgun and thinking, why are we wasting our time wrecking a car for no reason? The wheel came off, but we have business to take care of. He was doing so many drugs that he had sores all over his arms and was now picking at them all the time. He was already an arrogant, shameless pig. He was gross, and it was one more reason not to be around this creep.

That little voice that tried to keep me out of trouble wasn't saying run like it should have, or maybe I wasn't listening. On most of the trips to Mexico, Acree was doing his drugs and at night would put the boat on autopilot and go to sleep. I was so paranoid that I would sleep on top of the floorboards that covered the engine so that any change in the engine's rhythm would wake me up because I could handle any problems that needed fixing. One day when Paul was pulling in an Albacore, the little voice that protected me and said, "Grab that belt loop and toss that fucker into the ocean." But I'm not a murderer, and the little voice also said, "You're going to regret that."

Ugly Paul made a deal with Ugly Frank for us to bring three tons of Mexican weed into the USA, but first, we had to go to Punta Colonet and shoot off some flares to prove we could get down there and back. Paul and I fueled the Patrick at the Marine dock on Shelter Island and were off to Colonet.

MORE SPIT

Patrick was running pretty well. Paul was snorting something; I'm not sure what it was because I didn't want any. I like to be as straight as possible when putting myself at risk and hanging out with Paul since it was getting more perilous all the time. The trip to Colonet was uneventful, as we liked, but after we shot the flares, Acree had some of his dope blow out the window on the bridge. That was it for him; he had to lie down and now I'm driving the boat. A couple of hours later, the boat seemed to be slowing down. I went down to check the engine and the bilge and found the bilge was taking on water.

I woke Paul up, and we started to bail the water, but it was coming in faster than we could bail it out and we had to make a decision: we could drive the boat towards the shore in Mexico and let it sink, or call the Coast Guard. We choose the Coast Guard, but since Paul was on probation for crashing the Pantera while possessing two ounces of cocaine and a derringer, that was not going to be without peril.

An hour later a Coast Guard helicopter dropped us a huge gas-powered bilge pump. Soon after that, a Coast Guard cutter (ironically, it was the Point Stuart) showed up, took us off the boat, and towed us into San Diego Harbor. The captain of the Coast Guard Cutter wasn't friendly with us at all because it was pretty easy to figure out we weren't fishermen. Still, the captain did offer us showers, and I think was only because we were stinking.

SNAKREE

Paul had a rented house on Texas St. in North Park of San Diego. I crashed out there sometimes because I no longer had a home to live in. I was a true vagabond. One day, I was over there hanging out, and I had some excellent weed I'd gotten from Judy Jordan. She gets it a little before Christmas every year, and it was stinky. Probably the best Mexican weed I've ever smoked.

So I'm over at Texas Street smoking some weed, and Paul's all fucked up on God knows what and alcohol too. He's doing the usual asshole crap that he always does when he's fucked up, and someone called the cops. So, when the cops came, Paul goes out there and is all belligerent with them, and somehow he gets away with it. I went out there to try and calm things down, and they arrested me for being drunk in public when I hadn't even had a drink.

It was just a rouse, but I had an ounce of that really good weed in my front pocket, which was stupid, and they took it away from me. But they never charged me with possession of marijuana because that weed was too good to put in the police evidence room. I believe they just split it up. When I got booked at County Jail, I had fifteen hundred in my pocket, and they asked what my occupation was. I told them busboy.

I got a pretty strange look from the booking clerk and snickers from others getting booked. I'm sure they knew I wasn't a busboy. They kicked me out the following day, and I walked to the Coronado Bridge and hitchhiked to Coronado. Big Guy still had a house there, and I walked there; little brother let me in, and I called Paul to get me so I could get my car. He thought it was funny that I got arrested instead of him. I had a different opinion.

I'LL NEVER KNOW FOR SURE

A couple of weeks later, I was hanging out in Coronado when my best friend's sister showed up. She was looking for me in a nice late-model Mercedes and wanted to party. I was wondering where she got those wheels, but she wanted me to get a hotel room so we could party and she was beautiful and it was hard for me to refuse. It has been a while since I partied with her, but she and Betsy B used to come over to my beach cottage and partied with me many times before (Betsy was my favorite).

We got a hotel room at the Shoreland Motel and hung out for a little while, but I knew what she wanted and where to get it. She loved cocaine, and I knew that had to be part of the party deal, so we hopped in her Mercedes (it probably wasn't hers). I told my paramour that Paul was staying at the Sheraton on Harbor Island. It took us about fifteen minutes to drive there, and when we walked into the lobby, it was full of cops. It was like someone told them we were coming or they were listening to our conversation somehow; you could just smell them.

When we got up to Paul's room with my super sexy girlfriend for the night, I told him about all the cops in the lobby. He didn't seem concerned, but I was. When we were leaving, all the cops were still there, and I heard one of them say,

"Why aren't we arresting him?"

"Not them," an officer said.

I was worried now, and I thought Paul would get busted. He was on probation and had a bunch of dope—but now a little less cocaine than he had before we showed up.

He was all fucked up. I now had a big wad of it (never enough for the woman I was with, if past experiences were any indication). We went back to our hotel room in Coronado to party and have sex with my best friend's big sister. And she was gorgeous and a lot of fun too. She was best friends with another woman I liked even more. We had a great time, but it was weird.

I kept thinking about all those cops. It's like somebody clued them in about where Paul was (and they'd just got there, it seemed). It wasn't me, but it was like my conversation was known to the police. It makes me wonder if somebody else had gotten busted and now they needed someone bigger to take their place in the super-flawed criminal justice system. I'm pretty sure that's the night Paul Acree got busted. It would be the start of the downfall of the Coronado Company and many other people, including me.

FIVE PIECES OF SILVER

One day, when I was hanging out in Coronado, Acree called me and told me he heard Eddie O. had a million dollars at his girlfriend's house and planned on stealing it. The day before, I ran into Eddie at the beach. He took me to his girlfriend's house, pulled a large suitcase out from under the bed, opened it up, and said, "It's a million dollars; you want to count it?"

I'd been counting a lot of money lately and declined. Eddie was put out, but I told him, "I'm a little tired of counting money." He liked that.

The next day, Paul called me at the alley house and told me he had a crew flying to San Diego to take the million from Eddie and wanted me to see if Eddie was at his girlfriend's house. I went by his girlfriend's house and didn't see the Porsche, so I went to the beach and hung out in my car. I knew Eddie's routine. He usually drove by

Center Beach, then went down Alameda. I was there about fifteen minutes when Eddie saw me and made a U-turn.

I didn't let him get out of the car, and I told him what Acree was up to, and he made another U-turn and sped off. Then I returned to the alley house, called Acree in Santa Cruz, and told him his car wasn't there. I heard later from Paul that the crew arrived via private plane and couldn't find him, and that was good because I'm sure they would have killed him if they needed to, to get the million dollars. I always wondered how many people Eddie showed that money to, who they were, and who told Acree because it sure wasn't me.

PAUL ACREE GROWS EARS AND A TAIL

We had the Patrick berthed in San Diego Harbor now. We could berth anywhere we wanted because it was a U.S. documented boat, unlike most boats registered with the DMV in California.

A couple of weeks later, after our failure at Punta Colonet, Paul received a call from Lance, who told him some local smugglers had brought in a load of high-quality Oaxaca spears. They needed someone to handle distribution for them. I still had contact with the Washington guys, so I called one of them and told him I'd come across some special weed if they were interested. So, I flew up there and stayed at my buddy Chuck's house in Puyallup, a rural area outside Tacoma. I had probably been up there a dozen times, and Chuck was a great host.

He always found a pretty, horny girl for me. It was his girlfriend, I think, that set me up with the girls. After she met me, she told Chuck, "Let me know when he's coming back. I've got some girls for him." She had some lovely, sweet girlfriends, and they just came over and slept with me. They were all nice women, and they all mentioned how much they liked my tan, I always thought that was funny. I've never had a tan. I get redder in the sun, but everybody up there in the wintertime is white as copy paper.

It took a while for that load to arrive, and it came in a van and a truck. The guy in charge was Carlos. He also set up the Coronado Company with the tuna boats to bring in the thirty-plus ton loads. It left me wondering what I needed Acree and Lance for? I've known Carlos since I was a kid, and his parents were on my Evening Tribune paper route.

Chuck and I were preparing to leave Puyallup when I saw a Ford Victoria drive by. I mentioned that to Chuck because, in my eyes, a Ford Crown Victoria is a cop car. Soon, Chuck and I were on the road down to SeaTac airport, where there were lots of hotels and supposedly Carlos and the load were waiting for us. When we got there, I could see Carlos's van in the parking lot with another truck I recognized, too.

I got the number to the hotel room from Acree before we left Chuck's and I went up and knocked on the door with Chuck right behind me. When I walked in, there was Paul Acree and another guy I didn't recognize, which made me uneasy. Then I saw all the beer cans in the living room and asked him where Carlos was. Paul told me they all went out for something to eat. Then he had a big box of weed that looked nice. I would be the paymaster (all the money was going through me). I planned to end my relationship with Acree and take part of his money because it was owed to me.

I'd left my car with him when I left San Diego for SeaTac, and my clothes and stuff were at his Texas Street house, but he was up here now, and Chuck was stoked with the weed. We made plans to meet the next day to take the load off his hands. We walked back to Chuck's Corvette, and about twenty or thirty cops with guns jumped out, yelled, and screamed at us to get down on the ground, which we did, but I still had a cop put his gun right on the back of my head. I knew right then Acree had rolled over, the rat. Its one thing getting busted, but I felt terrible about walking my connection and friend Chuck into it.

We were in federal custody, but for some reason, we ended up in the King County Jail. I believe they were remodeling the federal lockup or building a new one or something like that. They put us in a cell with Carlos, George Roberts, and my two buddies, Kingfish and DC. I was sorry to see Kingfish there; he already had two felonies for smuggling, and my buddy DC, who was famous for surfing with his dog and also having a house in Coronado for twenty-two years at twenty-five bucks a month, I felt bad for them too; they shouldn't have been there. Still, it is what it is, and now we'll all have to face the music. Of course, the one guy missing in that cell was scumbag Paul Acree, the snitch.

The next day, they chained us (wrists and ankles) all up with a bunch of other guys and walked us from King County jail through the streets of Seattle to the federal courthouse. Then, later on that day they walked us back after our hearing. That evening, they served dinner and I still don't know what that was, but I know it was green and runny. I didn't eat, but Kingfish ate mine, too, as he had more experience eating institutional food than me. That evening there was a guy in the jail that kept yelling and yelling, and then we could hear him getting the crap beat out of him by the goon squad, and it lasted for about thirty minutes. I always wondered if that guy lived, died, or was taken to the hospital, but I know one thing: we never heard him yell again.

Our preliminary hearing was over, and our bail was set, so I called someone to whom I had given money and asked them to bail me out and pay for an airline ticket, which they did. I asked one of my friends if I could sleep in his small backyard and he was okay with it. Suddenly, I was pretty much broke. I gave Acree some money before I left, and he had my car, which disappeared (the pink slip was in my stuff at his house), with all my clothes at Paul the Snitch's house on Texas Street. You can never trust a junkie for any reason, and I was a fool for doing so, but I was still only twenty-two years old. Who knows what happened to our company money.

Paul had told me many stories about his Coronado Company days, but I shared none of those in this book. Still, I want to tell just one story because it's so funny.

The Company was smuggling by Zodiac to the Coronado Silver Strand. They had a small beach crew and two men in the Zodiac. When they hit the beach, two bright lights went on, and someone yelled, "Freeze! Police!" All the company guys, including the two in the zodiac, ran for it. The two guys with the lights jumped in the zodiac and sped off with the load. They later found the zodiac in north Imperial Beach minus the sea bags.

They had their suspects, and I'd agree with one of them, a guy named the Hulk. He was one crazy psycho who later proved that being a tweaker and being a type one diabetic isn't very good for your health.

STARTING AT THE BOTTOM AGAIN

A few weeks later Big Guy rolled into town. Paul had called and had him clean the Texas Street house, and I went over to the home off Fourth and J to talk to him. Big Guy said: "You still love Paul, don't you?"

"I never loved Paul. In fact, I want to kill him." But that wasn't my style, and I knew I'd never do it, but I still wanted to, and I thought someone would. Then I told him, "He's going to roll over on you and your brother too."

He wanted to debate that, but I didn't give him an avenue to do so.

He asked me where I was staying, and I told him I was sleeping in Big Al's backyard. A few months later, he returned to Coronado, he told me I could sleep on the couch at the J Street house. A few weeks later Big Guy showed up again, and this time, he brought a girl with him, a girl I knew well. She liked me, and I'd had plenty of sex with her, but she was never my girlfriend. One time, I found her in Coronado, and I had a bunch of cocaine that I got in from Paul. She and I ended up at the Holiday Inn in Mission Valley, where we made such a racket carrying on with our debauchery that they had to move all the people into rooms that were contiguous to ours. We had plenty of cocaine, and every time she thought we were done, I gave her some more. I banged her all night and into the morning when she told me she was getting sore and it was time to stop. And now she's got a bedroom in the alley house and I got the couch.

Big Guy left, returned to Santa Cruz, and left the girl at the J Avenue alley house. I didn't see Big Guy for a couple of years until we both ended up in a courtroom after Acree snitched us all off at the grand jury.

I asked him, "Do you still love Paul?"

And he said, "No, I want to kill him."

Back to the first bust. That late spring and summer, when I was going to court, Jenny would come out of her bedroom every night and give me a blowjob on the couch, and a good one at that. I should have treated her better. She was a really nice girl. She liked me and I liked her, but I knew I was going to prison. I didn't need a steady Betty or anyone waiting for me when I got out because I didn't know when that would be.

She told me I could be having much more fun with her. However, she was still kind of my ex-partner's girlfriend. It was his house, so for some reason, I thought that would be crossing the line, even though she was blowing me every day and I liked that and didn't want to give it up. But I was a dick, not that I was mean to her or anything. I just never gave or let her have the love she wanted from me. She was a good girl and stuck around all summer until our sentencing day in October.

THE SYSTEM

Regarding our problem with the criminal justice system, all the charges were dropped in Seattle and we were re-indicted in San Diego, all six of us. I got a call from an attorney named Pat. He told me that someone had paid for my attorney's fees and we made an appointment. I knew that would be the Coronado Company. They didn't want anybody spilling the beans. I wasn't about to snitch anyway, but they had other reasons too. Acree told me that Lance said they were about to go international and were not going to be smuggling kilo weed from Mexico. Now they were going after Thai weed and hash.

    I went to the attorney's office, where we previously met with Acree's attorney. It was also the office of Phil DeMassa and the attorney I played tennis with in a foursome with Judy Jordan. It's a small world sometimes; it can get even smaller. When I met my attorney, I instantly recognized him as someone who picked me up hitchhiking on Highway 395 in Balboa Park when I was in high school.

Back in Coronado, I'd gotten a job to please my probation officer, attorney, and court and to make myself look legitimate. Mr. Big Time was now bussing tables at a little French restaurant about a block and half from the Hotel Del Coronado named the Chez Loma. The two original owners had gotten into a fight. They were dissolving their partnership, and both ended up in the emergency room at Coronado Hospital. It was a real fight!

Darrel Deloach, the former lead singer in Iron Butterfly (he quit before "In-A-Gadda-Da-Vida" became a big hit), was the owner who got bought out. They had a waiter there named Jimmy Redline; another smuggler who worked as a boat driver for the Coronado Company and who did me the favor that no one else would in giving me a job.

I couldn't believe how many people were out there, for whom I did all kinds of favors that wouldn't give me the time of day or even a dishwashing job after I'd given them Thai sticks and all sorts of other stuff. Still, you find out who your friends are when you're down and out. A lot of people were trying to kick me at that time in my life. It's funny (not really) how many people acted like they were my friends when I was rolling in cash and now came to my face to put me down. I, of course, had no doubt this was temporary and that I'd be making a comeback.

THE SYSTEM

Jimmy Redline was a former U.S. Navy Seal who once played football with the Dallas Texans and the Kansas City Chiefs. He was a small college All-American before he got drafted to fight in Vietnam. He joined the Navy and became a Seal. He did three tours in Vietnam, the last two working for the CIA smuggling heroin from Burma to Thailand. One time he was being chased by customs while he was piloting a zodiac full of weed. He outran them that time and returned the zodiac and the weed to Mexico, but a few days later, they tried to bring the load in again. Customs was waiting for them in three boats, so he used a rope to tie off the zodiac so it would drive itself and he dove into the water and swam two and half miles back to land. Paul Acree and I got the whole story from a former agent, who was then a drunken harbormaster in Oceanside at the Joy Roger.

First, he told us how he took thirty kids out on a safety cruise as the Harbormaster, and a rogue wave sank the boat. Then he told us how they stopped the zodiac (when he was working for U.S. Customs) after Redline jumped off. We always wondered how they did it, and now we knew they used two other boats to get side-by-side on the zodiac until somebody jumped in. Redline told many stories when he was partying, and I heard that one several times.

One night, after working at the Chez, I went to a party on Coronado Avenue, and when I left, there was a cop car following me; they were waiting for me to come out of the party. A few blocks away, Officer Crook pulled me over, and he asked, "Stuart, I can help you?"

I told him, "I don't need any help, "

"Stuart, you'll end up in prison, and you'll have a record."

I said, "But I'll still be a man and not a rat."

"How much if you had to drink tonight?"

"Not a drop."

He nodded. "I'll contact you again in a few days."

I replied, "Don't bother."

I made it pretty clear that I wouldn't be turning state's evidence or making any deal. I was going to take my punishment like a man. He really thought he would have some leverage by catching me drunk driving, but I was one step ahead of him, and apparently he didn't know I'm not much of a drinker.

All six of us pleaded guilty. I forget what everybody pleaded to, but I and others pleaded to felonious use of an electronic communication device. We got the hanging judge, Gordon Thompson, who was known to be tough on defendants. I was set up to get a misdemeanor charge, and then suddenly, I got bumped into a felony. It was a side deal made not by me but by the attorneys working for the Coronado Company.

My buddy Chuck got four years and was indicted in Washington State for other stuff because of a different snitch. Kingfish got four years. He was lucky that mandatory minimums hadn't been dreamed about or implemented. Today he'd get life without parole for three marijuana felonies. If that doesn't seem right it's because it's not right. Carlos and I received four-year sentences and a chance for modification at the end of our ninety-day diagnostic studies. DC and George Robert got probation, as they should have. They weren't criminals, just guys looking to earn extra cash.

The four of us were sent immediately to MCC in downtown San Diego until Chuck and Kingfish went to Lompoc or Terminal Island. Carlos and I stayed at MCC for our diagnostic studies. After, Carlos and I were back in court, and the hanging judge let me go and kept Carlos for another month or two. Judge Thompson looked at me and said, "If I ever see you in my courtroom again, you can be assured I will give you the maximum I'm allowed to give you by law."

That was disturbing because I knew I would be back once Slimy Paul "The Rat" Acree got done testifying before the grand jury. After I was processed and about ready to be released, they put a hold on my release. I sat on a little bench for twelve hours before they released me and it was one in the morning during winter, and all I had on was a short sleeve polo shirt and I froze until my ride came to pick me up.

FINDING THE BOTTOM

Big Al told me I could stay at his house on Isabella in Coronado. It was a little house with only one bedroom, so I was sleeping in the living room but it was all right with me because I was free. The next day, I went to the Chez to see if Mr. Big Time could get his old busboy job back and found my old friend Nancy was working as a lunch waitress (my old pal who took care of me when I was a semi-homeless teenager). She gave me a big hug and asked me if anybody had taken care of me yet since I got out. I'm not stupid so I told her not yet.

She smiled and said, "I'll be off work soon."

We went over to Big Al's and rolled around on the floor in the living room for a couple of hours. It was more than just nice to see her again; that's what friends are for. After about a week, or maybe ten days of sleeping on Big Al's floor, he kicked me to the backyard, but I still had shower privileges. Talk about piling on. Some people were unbelievably mercilessly mean to me now when I was down. Still, I was only twenty-three and didn't plan to be down forever.

I got the part-time busboy job back at the Chez and had my pad, except it was outdoors. It was an El Niño winter, and it rained a lot, but lucky for me I had a much better sleeping bag than the old Boy Scout sleeping bag (Thank you, Pat), and I would pull it up over my head when it rained a lot.

It rained a lot that year.

I was in the backyard in the middle of the night. I was tired, but I couldn't sleep. I was thinking, here I had just turned twenty-three, I didn't have a high school degree, I just got a felony for smuggling weed, and another one was on its way, from all the things Acree and others were telling the grand jury; oh, and of course I was homeless.

I was biding my time when I heard Carlos was getting out of the can. My attorney called me at work the next day and asked if I could surrender at the federal courthouse on Monday. I guess I didn't have to worry about it anymore. It was here. I was basically broke. I had a few thousand dollars in a safety deposit box in North County. Acree had taken all the company money or lost it when he got busted. He stole my car, all my stuff, set me up, and ratted on me, too. I couldn't get much lower, and it seemed like people were piling on. That's how I got to find out about all the mean people who I thought were my friends, people I had done all kinds of favors for, and now I was down, and they had a chance to kick me, and they did.

And then it started to pour big drops of rain, so I pulled that sleeping bag over my head and told myself I needed to go to college and get a degree. It was 1978, the rainiest winter I could remember.

ROUND TWO

A few days after Carlos got out of the can, my attorney told me I needed to be in the federal courthouse on Monday at 9 o'clock. This was the second bust I knew was coming. The first one I got set up, and the second was from a grand jury where Paul Acree, the snitch, and some others testified against people who used to be their friends. I believe there were fourteen of us, fourteen out of twenty-seven named in the still secret indictment. The Magistrate called the court to order and then asked for a show of hands to see how many people were surrendering for the yet-unveiled secret indictment, and fourteen hands went up.

The indictment was no longer secret; it was in the news the next day. After about a year of wrangling, a deal was made. The Feds were going to walk us all, except Lou Villar, Lance Weber, and Ed Otero (who all remained fugitives) for guilty pleas. Bob Lahodny got a misdemeanor, and Carlos and I took the heavy hit with two felonies each. I always wondered how that deal transpired. I thought the hanging judge was going to hang me because he had previously told me he would and that was his reputation, but I walked, and I was never debriefed by the DEA either.

REDEMPTION

One morning, I was returning from the Laundromat, less than a block away, where I went every morning to dry out my sleeping bag. While there, I ran into Quita. Quita was an old friend. I'd known her since I was a little boy (my mom set me up to walk her to school every day when I was in first and second grade). She looked at me and said, "How are you doing, Stuart?"

"Pretty good."

She smiled and said, "I have an apartment that needs painting. It's empty, and you can sleep on the floor." She pulled the key out of her pocket and said: "You can start today." She gave me the address and said, "There's paint and supplies in the kitchen."

I told her, "Thank you."

Wow, just like that, I was out of the rain and the cold, I had work, and I was going to have a paycheck. But it was so much more than that. I had someone who loved and cared about me, and I had a restored faith in humanity. Thank you again, Quita. I love you.

I was done painting in about a week and I'm not sure the job was completed, but I was done. I knew long ago I wasn't suited for manual labor, even though I was strong as an ox; it just wasn't going to interest me. I was starting to pick up more busboy shifts at the Chez. I was back in Big Al's backyard, and the rain had abated a bit and I was more comfortable with my situation.

A month later, I was offered a car for one hundred dollars, and it had a huge back seat. I knew I'd found a new home and thought I could get girls back there, too, but I was dreaming. My love life wouldn't be back on track for a few more months. Then, one of the surfers Bros, found a cheap two-bedroom alley house and needed a roommate or was reaching out and being kind. I was off the streets and on the upswing, and finally, I had a place to take girls.

SOME THINGS NEVER CHANGE

It was 1987. I was working as the *maître d'* and head waiter at the Chez when I finally finished my finance degree at San Diego State University. My old friend CJ offered me a job in Hawaii on the island of Kauai, so I booked a flight. I didn't know if I would take the job, but it was time to reward myself with a nice vacation, and I love Hanalei. CJ supposedly had this thriving tourist business running people down the Na Pali coast in Zodiacs. Still, when I got there, the job I envisioned myself having was being worked by CJ's father.

That was all right. I wasn't disappointed. I didn't know if I would be taking the job in the first place, and it was nice to see some Hanalei people that I'd hung out with for a decade and a half now. CJ said he was going to a trade show on Oahu and had a place to stay there too. I just got a finance/business administration degree, so I decided to tag along and see what this was all about. While there, I met CJ's girlfriend; he was still married to a very nice girl that he left on Kauai. She was an interesting girl, and we hit it off right away. After the trade show, it was decided we would all fly to Maui. CJ's girlfriend and CJ went in the morning, and I flew over in the afternoon.

On the plane I was sitting next to Jay North, the kid who that played Dennis the Menace on TV when I was a boy. CJ picked me up at the airport, and we saw Dennis the Menace hitchhiking as we left. I told CJ that it was Dennis the Menace, and CJ said we were not picking him up. Apparently, he knew all about him. He told me he lived on a boat in Lahina harbor. We all decided to go to dinner at the Maui Chart House, where two guys from Coronado were the manager and the assistant manager.

My surfer buddy and spoiled brat friend Baby was the assistant manager. My old buddy Albert Earl Sweeney's stepbrother Pete Johnson was the manager and the future father of two of the most beautiful women in the world, Audrey and Delaine. I went to use the bathroom, and when I returned, CJ told me about the real job offer. It was a smuggling job, bringing Thai weed over on a sailboat, and they wanted to land the load with an amphibious assault. My job, if I were to take it, was to drive a Mark Five Zodiac, which can carry a ton of marijuana, from the sailboat through the surf in the dark of night onto the beach.

I immediately said, "That's not what I went to college for."

I could sense a strange feeling coming over me, an epiphany. I'd already come of age smuggling weed, I'd built more character than I would ever need, and I could feel myself heating up (turning red). I knew I was losing a friend, but what I didn't know was that I was gaining one too when CJ's girlfriend said, "I like your answer."

I worked so hard to rebuild my life, and my old friend didn't care one bit. He was willing to throw me right back in the abyss. I was disappointed in CJ, but a few days later, when we were back on Kauai, he told me that his girlfriend wanted to go out to lunch with me before I left for the mainland. We went out, but we only drank beer until it was time to go, and we kept up a relationship for years (I visited her and she visited me) until I had children with another woman. One of my friends took the smuggling job and made one hundred and eighty-five thousand dollars for three days of work and one night of smuggling. I could have used the money, but I'd promised myself and others that I'd stay out of the business, and I did.

THE PRIMROSE LABYRINTH

Sex, drugs, and rock and roll. Those were the days. I know many of you are smiling right now, and it was a lot of fun. Everyone got sucked in, we weren't living vicariously through someone. If you were cool and who didn't want to be cool, some of us got in a lot deeper than we even knew, and it happened so fast. There were lots of what today you would call influencers, fagens, users, and pied pipers whatever you would call them, pushers if you were street level. They all had their ways of pulling you into the labyrinth.

There were many ways to get lost or lose yourself and do things you never thought you would do in a thousand years. Some people died in there, and some are still wandering about in there, trapped. Not many of the deep dwellers ever made it to the surface or found their way out, and even if they did, they didn't know how to flourish or even take care of themselves in some cases. Nobody got out unscathed.

It was the seventies, and a revolution was going on. We were told one thing when we knew it was another, and things needed to change. Along with that came the drug culture, which wasn't as bad as people tried to make it out to be, but it did change and become more dangerous over time. It did begin as peace-love thing, and almost all the drug deals in those days were good, it was the good deal days (Hippies), but that came to an end with *The War on Drugs*. The government was at war against its people, and like all wars, there were lots and lots of casualties.

The War on Drugs and its war on the citizens ended the good deal days in favor of big business takeover, which became the Mexican cartels along with gringo or American smuggling operations. And for some reason, Mexican suppliers always had a soft spot for gringo smugglers. My journey started young and I tried to resist. I did resist years of people trying to coerce me into the business. However, as I got older the influence intensified. It was coming from teachers at the high school, my friend's parents, my employer, my landlord and my older (so called friends), along with doctors, lawyers, and other professional people who wanted to feel like they were in on it too. They wanted a piece of the Drugs, Sex, and Rock and Roll (who didn't?) along with the tax-free money that was a lure all its own. In the smuggling business, you're almost like a rock star, and you could undoubtedly party like one because you had the drugs, and with the drugs and the parties came the girls.

Then, the dark side came. Too much money was at stake, which changed people's behavior. They would routinely be doing things they never dreamed of themselves doing. Lots of people got sucked in, and almost everyone I know at one point in their lives could have willingly involved themselves in a catastrophic drug deal resulting in lengthy incarceration, the right time, and the right lure and they're in. We filled up the jails, prisons, and graveyards with people who deserved better.

Most have themselves to blame in a way, but society has a huge share of the blame as well. Their government's policy is wicked and perverse. Your children aren't your enemy, and all these victims were someone's children. A lot of their lives were wasted unnecessarily. The Coronado Company was glorified as local heroes and national legends. Still, they were a bunch of criminals who even had their own hitman.

Every principal in the company, past or present, rolled over and turned people in, making them all rats or snitches. There's no glory about them. They left Fred Stocker in a pit as collateral for payment for a load of hash and used that money to smuggle Thai weed. They didn't care about Fred; he was Lou's brother-in-law.

At one time, Fred was an excellent surfer in great shape and a super friendly guy, but by the time they got him unchained and out of his pit, he would never be the same. He could barely walk and didn't talk; they were heartless and cruel and didn't help him at all. Then there are all the people they corrupted and that list is longer than this book. It was the time when everyone got led down the primrose path and into the labyrinth. Most people, who think they're familiar with the story, think Lou Villar was the biggest pied piper. Still, he was coerced, with money, into the business by Lance Weber.

Most people in the business didn't fit the normal mold somehow, and once you're in it, so hard to change, and it was always party time, too. One day decades later I was at the swap meet in San Diego and ran into a young man who looked familiar. I asked him, "Do you know a guy named Stanley?" He chuckled and said, "I get asked that occasionally. Stanley's my uncle." Then he said, "How do you know Stanley?" I told him, "I met Stanley in Hanalei while in the marijuana smuggling business."

The young man asked me, "What are you doing now?" I told him," I got a finance degree and became a mortgage banker and real estate broker." He chuckled again and said, "You're one of the survivors."

I thought about that for a second. He was right. There are not a whole lot of survivors from *The War on Drugs*. There were casualties everywhere, including three of my lifelong closest friends, the kind of friendships and memories that just can't be replaced. I'm lucky to be alive and have had a good life because I never stop believing in myself.

POSTSCRIPT

In 1997, I bought a little house in Coronado, and in 2007, I decided to make it into a dream house and spent a million dollars expanding my home. We (my boys and their mom) rented a home in Coronado while this took place. Our across-the-street neighbor invited us to their Christmas party. While I was enjoying the party, their son came up to me and asked me who my judge was during my drug trials. I told him it was the hanging judge, Gordon Thompson.

A minute later, his mother came over to me, who had mothered one of my sisters after our mother was killed. She asked me to leave the party immediately. I was shocked, to say the least, but I decided I wouldn't make a scene, but I was going to leave my boy's mother at the party. Still, before I could get out the door, the judge stepped in front of me and kept me in a conversation for over forty-five minutes. He even wanted to play golf with me.

POSTSCRIPT

I would have to say he intentionally circumvented the intentions of the host. I later learned that the husband of the host family had lunch with him every week. That's when I figured out why we Coronado kids got such a good deal in Judge Thompson's courtroom. Thank you, Jack.